HISTORICAL SKETCHES OF
HARFORD COUNTY
MARYLAND

FIRST EDITION
250 COPIES

SUSQUEHANNA RIVER ABOVE ROCK RUN

HISTORICAL SKETCHES OF HARFORD COUNTY MARYLAND

BY

SAMUEL MASON, JR.

DARLINGTON, MD.

LITTLE PINES FARM

1940

INTELLIGENCER PRINTING CO., LANCASTER, PA.

THIS BOOK IS LOVINGLY DEDICATED TO
MY WIFE, WITHOUT WHOSE INSPIRA-
TION I SHOULD ACCOMPLISH LITTLE.

PREFACE

Flux and Change while unavoidable, are necessary to our real happiness and well being. But unfortunately as we get older, our retrospect is tinged with sadness, as we realize that those times are no more, and the prospects of the future are always appalling, for who can tell what it holds in store for us. It is natural therefore to attempt to bring back the past, by collecting memories before they become too hazy, and to present them to our families and others, that they may share them with us, and with this in mind, I am attempting to write, not a history, for this I have neither the inclination nor ability, but rather a series of sketches about our part of Harford County its activities and industries. Nor will there be any glorification of old families, as this is often a snare and a delusion. As to my sources: some are other books, some the memories of my friends and some my own memories; and if you think you detect errors, laugh and read on, as human nature is not always infallible.

CONTENTS

GRIST MILLS AND OTHER MILLS

UNRELATED SKETCHES

LIST OF ILLUSTRATIONS

INTRODUCTION

At first when a new strip of country is thrown open to settlement, the only report of the product is as crisply materialistic as a stock exchange report: so much of timber felled, so much corn and wheat and tobacco torn from that ground and shipped away; so much of wild-life displaced or slaughtered, and, instead, so many foundries, fisheries, cattle, hogs.

It is only when a soil has become permanently settled and its people truly civilized that it begins to grow human products of more enduring worth. These rolling hills and sheltered valleys of Harford County at the Chesapeake headwaters yield a great deal more than grain and livestock now. They yield ease, grace and serenity, legends and tales that rise above the Almighty Dollar and laugh about it, poems to this soil, eloquent singing and painting, unaffected but distinguished prose in the county papers, and books such as this.

I think this book is more than the author, in opening, modestly claims for it. It is more than a casual sketchbook quickly written. The parts link; the eye and mind are led from part to part in the light of a ripe understanding. We see why this headwater country of Old Harford, once cried up by boomers as a coming Pittsburgh, has become in the course of the years something entirely different, and a far more pleasant place of abode. This was largely because the farmers here did not want that sort of development. They did not want to boost and surge and scar the face of Earth. They had other aims and notions. They still have.

Samuel Mason, Jr., is a farmer in Harford County, and one of the best. He keeps reasonably up to date, but only reasonably so. He drives his own tractor and plows his own land, but plows less land now than ever before. Years before there was a Soil Conservation Service and an Agricultural Adjustment Administration in Washington, he had netted his crests with pines and had anchored his shoulder-land with meadows, to hold his soil. He farms sagaciously, taking time for other forms of cultivation, and leads a good life.

During the winters, especially, he pushes on into personal studies as a naturalist, mathematician, and anthropologist, quite on his own. Last winter he gathered together notes and memoranda that he had been for years collecting and considering, and wrote this book. He wrote practically all of it between the fall and spring, but the preparation took much longer. A long preparation is the greater part of writing well and simply and of getting at the truth.

RUSSELL LORD

"Thorn Meadow"
Harford County, Maryland
November 14, 1939

CHAPTER I

EXPLORATION AND EARLY SETTLEMENT

Captain John Smith.—It was early in August 1608. At the mouth of the Susquehanna, wind squalls were abroad, and the white caps licked along the sides of Captain John Smith's barge. The forest, from the very water's edge, undulated to the skyline in dense masses of wind tossed green and white, and in the occasional lulls, the derisive voices of the squirrels could be heard barking, although they themselves were out of sight. In such a setting Captain Smith first saw the famous Susquehanna warriors: sixty of them, who came from their fort two days journey up the river. The water was too rough for their canoes, and after receiving presents and homage, Smith took several of them across the bay to the Sassafras River in his barge, which was fitted with sails. A day or two of exploration, and he returned to Jamestown.

Palmers Island.—For fourteen years this wilderness remained undisturbed by white men. In 1622, however, a grant was obtained from the "Virginia Company of London," by one of its members, for a tract of land known today as "Watsons Island," opposite Havre de Grace. This man was Edward Palmer, an intellectual of Warwickshire, England. It is said that at a cost of many thousand pounds he prepared the island for a university, to be called "Academie Virginensis et Oxoniensis" where his sons among others were to be instructed in the higher branches of learning. "For the avoydinge of idliness," he provides as well instruction in "oyle and water cullors." Edward Palmer embarked in the fur trade as a means of promoting the

15

university and for that purpose is said to have settled
nearly one hundred men on the island or near it prior
to 1627.   Little is known of the project, which if it
existed at all, was short lived.   The island was known
as "Palmers Island" as early as 1637, but why its name
was changed to "Watsons Island," or who Watson was,
no one knows.

William Claiborne.—A vision that actually materi-
alized on this same "Palmers Island" a few years later
had its birth in the ambitious and insatiable mind of
William Claiborne.   Briefly, Claiborne had obtained a
permit from the Virginia Company for trading with
the Indians; and in 1632 was "squatting" on Kent
Island, as agent for a London Mercantile Company.
The relations of the company and agent were strained
from the first, as supplies from London were meagre
and the number of furs from Maryland did not come
up to the expectations of the company; for Claiborne
was evidently more interested in private venture.   But
private venture soon clashed with proprietary rights,
and when he captured a St. Mary's pinnace, trading
near the head of the bay, trouble really began.   It was
not long before he lost possession of the island, as the
London Company sent over its attorney, George
Evelyn, who explained the legal aspects of the case,
and forced Claiborne to flee.   The latter in 1637,
established himself on Palmers Island some forty miles
north, erected houses, built himself a fort and cleared
enough land to plant corn.   But even here he was not
secure, for the Island was well within the boundaries
of Lord Baltimore's domain, and early the following
year, agents of the latter arrived and confiscated
Claiborne's entire property.   Claiborne, as far as this
sketch is concerned, now drops out of the picture as he
returned to England.

We now find Palmers Island, in use in April 1643, as a center from which Lord Baltimore attempts to dominate the Susquehannock Indians. Ten good men are established here, with powder and shot and necessary supplies. They built a house and erected a fort, which was said to have stood on the South side of the hill, and on the North end of the Island. There was in all probability, a windmill on the hill top for use in grinding their corn, as there was one on Kent Island and no mention is made in the inventory of their goods at Palmers Island, of any hand mill. The island in more modern times, seemed to have been necessary to the Baltimore and Ohio Railroad as a stepping stone across the River. It has been farmed with the usual success, and now overgrown with trumpet creeper and dewberry vines, is ripe for advancement, as a modern concrete highway is soon to cross it.

Spesutia Island.—Although "Spesutia," like Watsons Island, is situated in Cecil County, my narrative would be incomplete, if I failed to include it. The island is situated in the bay just below Havre de Grace and was known to the Dutch previous to 1652 as Bearsons Island. Its present name of Spesutia, was due to its redoubtable owner Captain Nathaniel Utie; spes meaning hope in Latin.

Captain Utie was the most prominent pioneer at this time at the head of the bay. He came from Virginia, where after some political squabble his land was confiscated and he removed to Spesutia. He had with him a license permitting him to trade with the Indians and with the power to arrest anyone found trafficking about the mouth of the Susquehanna River. He was, in spite of his troubles in Virginia, again made a councillor of the Virginia Colony, one of their meetings being held on the island in 1661. At this council, he petitioned the members to pardon his former irregularities, which they agreed to do. In this same year on May 13th, the Maryland Council also met here, to discuss ways and means of holding the Indians in check.

Captain Utie lived on this island with his relative George Utie, who was as crossgrained and arrogant as his brother. Nathaniel also owned land at the mouth of the Gunpowder and in addition some more across the bay on the Sassafras River.

There is a story of six Dutch deserters which while having little to do with Harford County, seems interesting in view of the future boundary lines of the State of Maryland.

From time to time, Swedes and Finns left the Dutch settlements along the Delaware, and growing tired of Dutch rule, made their homes further South. Among these were six Dutch soldiers. The Dutch authorities at New Amstel being apprized of this, wrote a letter to the Governor of Maryland demanding their return. Not knowing however the whereabouts of the Governor, but being familiar with Spesutia Island and Captain Utie, they sent their demands to him to be forwarded. Utie however did not waste time communicating with the Governor, but accompanied by a few friends and the six deserters, made his way to New Ampsel arriving on September 6, 1659. He promptly surrendered the deserters and then in a boisterous, stormy manner, insisted that the Dutch abandon the town immediately, as it was situated within the precincts of Lord Baltimore's claim, which extended to the 40th parallel. The Dutch were much alarmed and immediately dispatched word to Stuyvesant at New York.

A meeting of the Governor and Council of Maryland was being held at Patuxent later in the same year, when two representatives of Governor Stuyvesant appeared on the scene, by name Augustine Herman and Resolved Waldron. These men presented a letter, which deplored the friction between the two colonies and hoped that the representatives and the Council of Maryland could reach some amicable understanding. The Dutch representatives, both very astute men, soon pointed out to the Maryland Council the one weak spot in the Maryland Charter, which was, that the Lord Proprietor was vested with a country not previously inhabited except by Indians and the land along the Delaware had been inhabited by the Dutch before the Charter had been issued. Thus Maryland lost all claim to the land between the Chesapeake Bay and the Delaware River.

Lapidum. (The Place of Stones.)—Six years pass, and the throb and roar of the Susquehanna, from countless riffles and rapids glistening up-stream, hold a menace for those traveling in canoes or small boats. The forest on both sides, has encroached as far as it dares on the water and great gnarled water birches line the banks as their descendants do today. Festoons of fox grapes hang from the trees on the larger islands, and cardinal flowers four feet high along the banks amaze and delight the beholder. At this time it was none too safe to leave the river, as there was a village of Indians up Herring Run on top the hill, besides several others in the immediate neighborhood.

Such was the condition when in September 1665, Thomas Griffith appeared from the direction of Havre de Grace, sailing up river. He first landed on the Cecil County side and admired the hill known later as "Mount Ararat" below Port Deposit. He then turned West and approached the Harford Shore somewhere near where the old Ice houses used to stand a

half mile below the Virdin property. Here there is a
small stream flowing through a tangle of bushes and
nettles on a comparatively level piece of land, and it
was at this point on the river, and at a large Spanish
Oak that he determined to begin the survey of his
patent known as "Eightrupp." The party no doubt
ate their lunch here and then began the survey. This
extended 250 perches up the river to a "pohickory,"
which stood near the present lock at Lapidum and
thence back into the woods 320 perches. In all enclosing 550 acres. None of these lines, other than the
one along the river were surveyed, as no one in the
party had the temerity to tempt the silent forest by
entering it. Griffiths obtained his patent on September 26, but later lost it, as he failed to settle on the
property within the time limits specified by law.

The first man who apparently had nerve enough to
actually settle on the site of Lapidum was one, Daniel
Johnson. He lived in 1698 on Spesutia Island, but
shortly after moved to his property here. He owned in
all about 100 acres. It extended from the beginning
of "Eightrupp" at the Spanish Oak up the river to
Herring Run; then up this to the "Old field," a former
Indian village and back again to the Oak. He cleared
some land and planted tobacco, wheat and corn and
he owned considerable livestock. After his death in
1715, an inventory was taken of his personal property,
which included: one short bodied coat, one hat, one
pair stockings and one branding iron. As for livestock
he had, four horses, fourteen steers, seven cows, four
calves, one heifer, nine sheep, forty-two young hogs,
and twenty-seven shoats; one cart, one plow, two axes,
one spade, one hoe, one grindstone and a hand mill;
also three old books. He left in addition, four thousand
pounds of tobacco.

At this time, there were no Susquehannock Indians in these parts, as they had been encouraged to move on previous to 1675 and those remaining, lived further up the river. There were however, roving bands of Indians of other tribes; such as the Shawnees, Nanticokes, and Delawares, who drifted in, after the Susquehannocks had moved out, and who, even in 1715 gave the early settlers about Lapidum, many an anxious moment.

"The Land of Promise," a tract of 2000 acres at the Northern end of "Eightrupp," was patented in 1684 by Colonel Thomas Taylor. His agent on checking up the survey, discovered that a large section had been inadvertently located in the River.

During the next fifty or sixty years, the country back from the river and up the Deer Creek, gradually became settled and Lapidum did comparatively little in the way of change during this time. She had her ferries, of which I will treat later, but nothing in a big way was done here until 1760. In that year, Reuben Perkins erected a stone grist mill, which stood on the North side of Herring Run. He operated this for ten years and then sold it to Nathaniel Giles, who owned at that time, the entire river front from here to the mouth of the Deer Creek. Giles previously had built a grist mill on Rock Run and no doubt bought out Perkins Mill in order to eliminate competition. Giles lived at Lapidum until his death in 1775, happily escaping the trials incident to the Revolution.

Herring Run was then for the larger ships, the head of navigation and thus a minor real estate boom began in the expectation of increased foreign outlet; land along the river front was sold off in half acre lots, which were purchased, many of them, by influential men. Four of these were Benjamine Rumsey, Aquila Hall, William Husband and Ebenezer Mackie.

In 1772, Jacob Giles built a large stone warehouse
North of the mouth of Herring Run for the use of the
Cumberland Forge operating then on the Deer Creek
above Stafford. He not only used it for supplies for
the Forge, but also as a storage station for the produce
of his several farms. Twenty-two years later (1794)
John Stump purchased this warehouse when he became
owner of the Cumberland Forge and made use of it
for storing pig iron, and also grain and flour, manufactured at his mills both at Rock Run and at
Stafford.

The real estate boom beginning in 1772 definitely
ended in 1808, in the sale of the remaining lots along the
river front. These were sold at an average price of
sixty dollars an acre. Other activities of river life,
will be dealt with hereafter, and we will now allow
Lapidum to enjoy her repose after the boom, while we
turn our attention to other matters.

The "Freelances," such as had been settling on the
lower river in the latter half of the seventeenth century,
had approached from the South from the more thickly
populated sections along the Bay. Law and order had
here begun to put restraint on the inhabitants. In a
community where there are comparatively few people
and where land is cheap, personal conflicts are few; but
as population increases laws seem to become necessary.
I say seem to become necessary, for I sincerely believe
that if every person faithfully followed his conscience,
and each went half way or further with the other,
there would be little need for lawyers; perhaps it is
fortunate for them that crime exists; but shouldn't
crime be rather encouraged than treated so harshly?
The same reasoning holds true for doctors. If the laws
of hygiene were obeyed would there be as great a need
for this profession? Be this as it may.

Baltimore on Bush.—In the year of our Lord 1674, a courthouse was authorized to be constructed on the East bank of the Bush River and two years later, the proprietor ordered the building of various Inns for the accommodation of the public near the Courthouse. Thus the "Seat of Baltimore County," which included at that time Harford County, had its birth and was named "Baltimore on Bush," which was certainly an appropriate name. Times were uncertain and Indians were plentiful and it is not hard to visualize an officer standing on the Courthouse steps and announcing to the assembled villagers, that three shots fired within fifteen minutes from the Courthouse door was to be a signal that Indian danger was imminent, and was to be answered from house to house throughout the Hundred.

William Osborne owned land in the town and was said to have built the first house. He was also enterprising enough to have owned a ferry which conveyed persons across the Bush. Philip Philips actually operated the ferry and finally bought it outright. Osborne's eldest son had the misfortune to have been stolen at one time by the Susquehannocks; they were pursued across the bay but without success and the boy was never recovered. Some years later an old Indian told the father that the boy had been well treated and had become a kind of chief and was said to have been one of the signers of the treaty between William Penn and the Indians in 1682.

One of the last records made at the Court House of "Baltimore on Bush" was in 1692. This was a suit brought by Thomas Heath, an innkeeper, claiming for tobacco due him for boarding the Justices during the years 1687, 1688, and 1689. Do not suppose for a moment, that these Justices did nothing but smoke tobacco; far from it; tobacco was then used as legal tender. The courthouse which was of wood, fell into disrepair in 1683 was offered for sale and the County Seat after a certain interval moved to Joppa. Trees and bushes encroached on the fields and finally even the cellar walls became levelled, so that as early as 1773 the site was known by tradition only and called "The Old Plantation." The march of progress, with the help of soldiers, has so altered this old site, that now practically all that remains is an old wood-road and a solitary grave slab, covering the remains of James Philips and his wife.

Old Joppa.—Today the traveller approaches "Old Joppa," along a narrow dirt road on the East bank of the Gunpowder River. At the point where the road ends, there is a large brick house, known as the Rumsey House, which is all that remains of the town of "Old Joppa." There is to be sure a ragged orchard, cellar holes here and there and also traces of a dock near the mouth of the Gunpowder and perhaps a gravestone or two in the graveyard; but nothing more. Why have these towns been abandoned? For beauty, the sites cannot be excelled. Was it because of a gradual silting of the water channels, or because the center of population was shifting, or possibly a combination of these reasons? The town site was chosen as one offering facilities for the shipping of tobacco and the project was given impetus, as was done by King David in Bible times, by condemning another's property. Colonel James Maxwell was a minor when the land was forced from him in 1712.

Nevertheless a prison was erected and a Court House, where governmental duties commenced. In ten years the commissioners had succeeded in legalizing their title and had drawn up plans for a town. This was

limited to twenty-one acres; the Odd acre being given
to the Lord, and on which, was erected St. Johns Par-
rish Church. The other twenty acres were sold off in
half acre lots, abutting on the four streets of the town.
East and West, extended Court Street and Church
Street; intersecting these and running North and
South, were Low Street and High Street. The lots
sold at the price of 1 Pound and 7 Shillings each, and
to be paid to Colonel James Maxwell. The require-
ments of the purchasers were rigid. Each owner was
to build himself a dwelling, covering not less than four
hundred square feet, (20' x 20') with a good chimney
built either of brick or of stone. "Old Joppa" was a
center for tobacco export, the plant was grown extensively all about; and required a rich soil, which was
easy to find in those early days, but after a century of
cropping, the settlers found it dwindling off, as com-
mercial fertilizer was unknown and fresh ground was
then not available. The town maintained for a time
a throbbing trade with Europe and the West Indies,
as large ships could sail directly to their docks for
loading. The rich soil that Old Joppa looked for in
vain to carry on her tobacco culture, can now be found
lying at the dock and all the way down the Gunpowder River, washed from our farms farther back in
the country.

At the time Philadelphia was settled in 1682, a number of grist mills were established on some of the
streams near that town. By 1740, sixty years later,
many of them had to close down owing to the shortage
of water. This was not due altogether to drought or
deforestation, as the latter had not been carried on
extensively enough. I believe the water table even at
this early date was beginning to subside. Another

example of a subsiding water table, is shown in the journals of Augustine Herman and Resolved Waldron, who as before mentioned, made the journey from New Amstel to Patuxent. On their way from New Amstel, instead of traveling South as we should do today to reach the Elk River, they instead made a wide detour to the North and West, in order to avoid a large swamp. Where is this swampy tract now? Our government has made extensive surveys of Mid-Western wells. In eighty wells examined, a subsidence of something like fourteen feet in the water level in twenty-eight years was discovered, or a drop of six inches a year.

But back to "Old Joppa." In 1731 on one of the return cargoes unloaded at the dock, was an out and out case of smallpox. This even now is a very serious disease, and it was so serious then, that the legislature passed a bill closing the Court House and suspended their sittings there for the time being. No doubt a number of the inhabitants died from the disease, as there was nothing else for them to do. The sanitary precaution of breathing through a handkerchief moistened with vinegar, was hardly enough to hold the disease at bay. However some must have survived, for the town as a Baltimore County Seat, continued to hold court here until 1768, when popular opinion caused it to be removed to Pikesville near Jones' Falls, thus removing the county seat permanently from Harford which became a separate County in 1774 six years later, as the inhabitants on the Susquehanna could not possibly endure the inconvenience of the long trip to Baltimore.

Harford Town.—In an old book in my possession, called "The Travellers Directory" printed in 1804,

there is a road map showing the new seat of Harford
County. It is apparently located on the flat, half way
between James Run and Bynums Run at Bush. The
Philadelphia Road passed through the town and there
seems to have been only one cross street. There are
shown fourteen houses and a grist mill, which was
located toward the junction of the two streams. Harford Town as a county seat, did not survive more than
eight years. During that interval however, crime
seemed to have been rampant, as in August 1774,
eighty-nine cases were included in the docket. How
the court existed without a jail, is hard to say, but none
was built, although plans for a commodious structure
of 20' x 20' was drawn up. All this time the need for a
jail became more and more pressing. A number of
suitable sites were suggested and dismissed, until
finally on April 27, 1782, Bel Air was unanimously
chosen as the obvious location.

Those locations deemed unsuitable, included Harford Town itself, Otter Point, Gravelly Hill, Churchville, and even Havre de Grace. Before the court
moved from Harford Town, it had committed itself in
writing, to the following "Declaration of Independence," which appeared more than a year before the
famous one signed in Philadelphia.

"We the Committee of Harford County, having
most seriously and maturely considered the Resolves
and Association of the Continental Congress, and the
Resolves of the Provincial Convention, do most heartily
approve of the same and as we esteem ourselves in a
more particular manner intrusted by our constituents
to see them carried into Execution, we do most solemnly
pledge ourselves to each other, and to our country, and
engage ourselves by every tie held sacred among man-

kind, to perform the same at the risque of our lives and
fortunes."

Signed,

Aquila Hall	Wm. Fisher, Jr.
Carvel Hall	Richard Dallam
Geo. Patterson	John Durham
Wm. Morgan	James McComas
Frans Holland	Wm. Bradford, Sr.
Sam'l Caldwell	Wm. Smithson
Aquila Paca	Jno. Donohuy
James Lytle	Jno. Patrick
Aquila Hall, Jr.	Daniel Scott
Robt. Morgan	Benj. Bradford Norris
Robt. Lemmon	James Harris
Thos. Brice	Edw. Prall
Thos. Johnson	Greenberry Dorsey
Alex Rigdon	John Archer
Edw. Ward	W. Smithe
Abm. Whitaker	W. Webb
Chas. Anderson	Jno. Taylor.

March 22, 1775

Harford Town in the year 1798, contained sixteen
dwellings, one hundred and thirty habitants, a cooper-
age, a grist mill, a tanyard, two taverns, a wheelwright
shop, a blacksmith shop and two storehouses.

Bel Air.—Having made the above declaration of
Independence, an agreement was signed, by which
Aquila Scott of James, conveyed to the aforementioned
Town Fathers on April 27, 1782, two and five-eighths
acres of land, for the site of the New Court House and
Jail at Bel Air. This and the immediate environs, was
locally known as "Scotts Old Field," and was purchased
for the sum of 22 Pound, 6 Shillings, 3 Pence, or about
one hundred and ten dollars at the present rate of

exchange. Scott's dwelling, torn down about 1930, was a weatherboard house having a hip shingled roof, a brick chimney at each end, and stood alone in a small field near the railroad and some distance behind the present oil storage plant at the North end of Bel Air. Six years after the date of the above conveyance, a Court House was erected approximately on the site of the present one and was of brick with wings to the North and South. The Court itself, occupied a large room with a brick floor and with two enormous open fireplaces, where cordwood was kept constantly burning in cool weather. The second floor, was reached by an outside stairway ascending from the front door towards the South, with a landing at the top, from which landing and stairway, political speeches were often made to those collected below. The jury rooms were on the second floor and the jurymen had to leave the warm room below and climb from outside to the chill of the upper regions, where we may imagine their unanimity occurring in a very short time, particularly in winter. A jury room should never be too comfortable.

The town contained in 1798, one hundred and fifty-seven inhabitants; of these thirty-six were colored. There was a Methodist Meeting House, four inns, three stores, two blacksmith shops, one chair maker, one shoemaker, one wheelwright and a tailoring establishment and in addition, the jail and the Court House.

On the night of February 19, 1858, a fire destroyed the center part of the Court House, but all records were fortunately preserved. A completely new building arose the next year, like the Phoenix from the ashes of the old; this piece of legerdemain was consummated by C. Coleman Smith, where it stands today, the pride of the just and the terror of evildoers.

CHAPTER II

FRONTIER FORTS AND BORDER TROUBLES

In Algonkin Indian mythology, according to Wm. B. Marye, the serpent has always represented the Evil Spirit and cloaked in feathers implies bravery. The Evil Spirit invariably lived under the water which was no doubt an excellent place for him to remain; however he required from the Indians constant propitiation, either in the form of tobacco scattered on the water or prayers or possibly serpent representations on rocks near his place of abode. This Evil Spirit quite positively made his headquarters in the deepest part of the channel locally known as "Job's Hole" at Conowingo and it is not to be wondered that certain island rocks in the River near here are covered with strange serpent-like carvings. Those located above the new power dam are of course now flooded.

On one of these rocks is an engraving of something like a fish with whiskers on each side. This rock was located directly under the Harford County end of the old Conowingo bridge and could formerly be seen there at low water. Other rocks projecting from one of the sunny islands below the mouth of Broad Creek were covered with concentric circles a foot in diameter, possibly representing nests or coiled serpents. Others were something like fish with three eyes and equipped with bristling whiskers; but whiskers as every woman knows, rarely denote bravery rather foolhardiness, these carvings therefore must represent feathered serpents, which logic is certainly unassailable.

In early times according to tradition, the Indians had built a fish pot immediately below the mouth of Broad

INDIAN CARVINGS AT THE BALD FRIAR ROCKS

Creek. It was constructed of large heavy stones in the
form of a letter V with the point downstream and in
recent years it had been repaired and used by white
men for the same purpose, a small wooden building
perched on the lower end to house the fisherman. The
writer was once trapped in this fish pot himself as the
canoe once in, could find no way out; the water cascad-
ing over the large stones along the V with deep water
both inside and outside but not deep enough on top to
float the canoe over. The Evil Spirit at this particular
time was not propitiated but strongly invoked.

A short distance above these rocks, was the site of
the Bald Friar ford. This ford in Indian times, was
used by the Delawares in crossing the river on their
hunting trips between the Susquehanna and the Potomac, and on the hill above the Harford end of the ford,
tradition also states, stood a stockade or fort. The site
of this fort is behind the first bald spot on Bald Hill,
enclosing a spring, which has now almost dried up.
From this eminence a clear view could be had of the
entire breadth of the river and if a long line of Indians
was seen, winding steadily across toward the Harford
Shore, an alarm was sent out by "Heralds," summoning
the inhabitants to the fort. It was known locally as
the "Old Indian Fort." It was palisaded and about
120 feet square. In Mr. Preston's "History of Harford
County," I notice that Captain Thomas Richardson,
was commander of the fort on the Susquehanna. Hauducoeur, who was employed by Lafayette as surveyor,
prepared in 1799, a map of the lower river. On this
map is shown at Bald Hill, a group of buildings with
the words "P. Fort." Could this mean "Primitive
Fort," or "Pioneer Fort"? In 1799, there would be no
use here for the fort as a protection from the Indians
but it may have been in a ruinous condition, although

still standing at that time. Beginning just below
Conowingo Falls and continuing to within a quarter of
a mile of the new power dam, is a strip of water fifty
or sixty yards wide, that runs swift and deep, with
gliding whirlpools forming and disappearing as you
watch them. I used to watch them through cracks in
the floor of the old Conowingo Bridge. This stretch of
water is known as "Job's Hole," and was believed to
be bottomless, until the Conowingo Power Company
put an end to the doubt by soundings, which recorded
a depth of approximately eighty feet. There was also
believed, at one time, to be an underground connection
with the Potomac or lower bay, as shad have been
caught up the Susquehanna before they were caught
further down. Actually the bottom of "Job's Hole"
above the site of the dam, is several feet below sea level.

Mason and Dixon's Line.—It is unfortunate that often
those who strive to follow the dictates of their con-
sciences, find themselves actually following the dictates
of their purses. The time has now arrived when the
famous boundary dispute between Pennsylvania and
Maryland must once more be brought to light, as on
this, necessarily depends the division of Harford and
York Counties and in order to be able to form a more
intelligent opinion, I shall give a brief summary of the
charters of the two Proprietors, William Penn and
Cecilius Calvert. Lord Baltimore's charter comes first,
and its bounds are quite plain. It was signed by King
Charles the First, on June 20, 1632 and embraces the
following points:

All land bounded on the North by the 40th parallel
of latitude; on the South by the South bank of the Potomac River; on the West, by the meridian passing
through the most extreme source of the same river,
and on the East, the Atlantic Ocean, provided the land

be previously unsettled, not including Indians. The
40th parallel of latitude incidentally, passes to the
North of Philadelphia and crosses the Susquehanna at
Columbia.

To William Penn, on March 4, 1681, was granted by
King Charles the Second, the following territory:

All that land bounded on the East by the Delaware
River, beginning at a distance of twelve miles North of
New Castle; on the North by the "Beginning of the 43d
parallel"; on the West, by the 5th degree of longitude,
on the South, by the "Beginning of the 40th parallel,"
on the Eastern end of which, it is to intersect the twelve
mile radius circumscribed about New Castle. The Duke
of York who conquered the Dutch in America in 1664,
owned this New Castle section and that part, down to
the mouth of the Delaware Bay at Cape Henlopen,
where there had been Dutch settlements as early as
1630. The Duke, being the King's brother, also deeded
his land to William Penn the following year, and for a
certain consideration. Penn's charter was based on a
petition which he had previously made to the King,
wherein he had visualized himself as the proprietor of
a port on the Chesapeake and believing that the 40th
parallel of latitude would include such a section on the
bay, was disgruntled to find it came much farther
North. He immediately began cudgeling his wits for
a means of fulfilling his desires and finally stumbled on
the words in his charter the "Beginning of the 40th
parallel." The "Beginning" would seem to mean the
39th parallel! This passes near Baltimore. All this
time the Calverts had not been idle and they insisted
that their land extended to the 40th parallel, as indeed
their charter stipulated. The Delaware section was
relinquished by them long before this, as Augustine
Herman and Waldron had made it clear to Nathaniel

Utie, that the Delaware territory had been settled by
the Dutch previous to the date of Calverts charter and
therefore Maryland had no claim to it at all. But
Maryland made it plain to Penn, that if the beginning
of the 40th parallel was considered the 39th, then at his
Northern boundary, the beginning of the 43rd parallel,
really meant the 42nd, where it is today and not at
Syracuse, New York. The battle raged furiously during
the lives of the proprietors and was kept hot by their
descendants for a hundred years until finally from sheer
exhaustion the problem was settled by a mutual petition to the King, that he in his wisdom might bring
the dispute to an end by establishing a suitable boundary line. This was consummated in 1738 by a temporary
line, which stood until 1750. The settlement made by
the Chancellor, was in brief as follows: First, a twelve
mile radius to be circumscribed about New Castle, with
its center at the court house. Secondly, an East and
West line to be surveyed from the most Easternly part
of Cape Henlopen to the Chesapeake Bay. From the
center of this, a straight line to run towards the North,
so as to form a tangent with the New Castle circle.
Thirdly, from this tangent point, a due North line
should be run to a point fifteen miles South of the most
Southern part of Philadelphia, and then fourthly, from
here a line extended due West as far as the two prov-
inces extended. In September 1766 Mason and Dixon,
the surveyors chosen for this task, having surveyed due
West, one hundred and sixty-two miles, were forced to
abandon their work as the Indians had ordered them to
proceed no further, and it was not completely finished
until 1789, having been in the meantime entrusted to
David Rittenhouse, the mathematical paragon of
Philadelphia.

Border Troubles.—It was quite natural for settlers along Maryland's Northern border, in these troublesome times, to feel uneasy and uncertain as to what they had best do. For as the verbal battle waged between the two proprietors, the allegiance of the settlers shifted from Maryland to Pennsylvania and back again as the arguments seemed to favor first one side and then the other. Allegiance, consisted in the payment of taxes to one state and the refusal to pay them to the other. There were many cases of armed thugs and bandits descending on farmers near the border, burning their homes and driving them one way or another and making their lives generally miserable. The leaders of these crews of wreckers were considered heroes on one side of the line, and border ruffians on the other side. Character seems to have been thus relative to a supposititious line and to be damned or blessed accordingly.

Frontier Forts.—There were however, certain inhabitants called "Border Ruffians" by both Pennsylvanians and Marylanders and these were the Indians. I hesitate to enter a long philosophical discussion, though I cannot help but think that these so called Ruffians, were merely defending their homes and attempting to drive out the pickets who were preventing or making impossible their livelihood in hunting. From the white man's point of view they were ruffians and formidable ones at that.

In 1692, Governor Copley of Maryland was informed that a war party of some eight hundred Indians was descending upon the Maryland frontier with torch and rifle. He instantly ordered the erection of a line of forts from the Patapsco at Elk Ridge, to the Susquehanna, a distance as the crow flies of fifty miles. The only one of these forts remaining today is on the property of Mrs. Charles J. Moore, near the Worthington Valley. It was so situated because two Indian trails intersected at this point, one going into Baltimore and the other continuing to the South. The old building called "Garrison Forest Fort" is of stone, and consists of one large room, twenty by fifty feet with a fireplace at one end; the chimney built inside the room and not outside, as is customary in these parts. Around the walls are slits through which the riflemen could shoot when occasion required. At one end up in the gable, is a door, which is said to have been at that time the only means of entrance; this being gained by a ladder which could be pulled inside. The roof was much steeper in those days than now, as it has been remodeled, and there were flagstones placed on it as a prevention from the fire from burning arrows. Near the end of the fort and now a part of Mrs. Moore's dwelling, was a small building used in those days for housing the friendly Indians, who acted as scouts and who kept the fort supplied with fish and game. They were supplied with certain articles of clothing in part payment. Another of these forts was said to have stood somewhere on "Fox Saw Mill Branch," which was once called "First Cabin Branch," this stream has its source near the Joppa road. The next fort was supposed to have been located on "Bear Cabin Branch" near Forest Hill and the site of the Eastern one is unknown, although any fort not immediately on the Susquehanna River would be comparatively useless and I should place it on Bald Hill above the Bald Friar Ferry, where as has been already mentioned was a "Susquehanna Fort" commanded by Captain Thomas Richardson.

Governor Copley, besides building these forts, organized a company of "Rangers." There were twenty of them, allowing five for each fort, and these men patrolled the line between the forts and were instructed to make note of anything of unusual interest and report this to the governor. These special reports, contained nothing of unusual interest as you might easily imagine. The pay of the Rangers was usually some months overdue and even their supply of powder and shot was barely sufficient.

In regard to guns, I was informed by the caretaker at Fort Ticonderoga, New York in 1936, that "Firelocks" and "Matchlocks" were in general use up to the year 1640. "Flintlocks" then came in, using a tough brown flint imported from England. These pieces of flint were fastened to the hammer which when released, scraped down along a piece of spring steel, deluging the priming with sparks and thus firing the gun. Many of these worn out flints which were discarded, have been picked up on Indian village sites and elsewhere. "Flintlocks" were in use as late as 1840, when "Percussion caps" made their appearance. Owners of flintlock guns could, at slight expense, have them changed into percussion cap guns. These later were used for approximately forty years, when in the 1880's the modern "Pin fire" guns were put on the market and 1880 thus marks the beginning of the end of game, such as ruffed grouse, in Harford County. The last one seen by the writer, was on Bald Hill about 1920. Percussion Cap guns were of two kinds. The tube which conveyed the fire to the powder in the charge, could be bought with a fine bore or a coarse one. When guns having the coarse bore tube were fired, the powder from the charge worked into the tube and a longer interval elapsed after the hammer fell, than if a tube of small bore had been used; as in the former case, the fire in the tube traveled from grain to grain of the powder and in the latter, the

percussion cap exploded directly through the tube into
the powder in the charge. Loons which are notoriously
hard to kill, could not be killed at all with rifles of the
large percussion tube style, as at the slight puff of the
cap, the loon dove. With those rifles equipped with
the small bore percussion tube, the flash of the cap was
almost instantly followed by the explosion of the charge
and the loon had less chance for escape.

The line of Rangers stations, probably did not exist
much over ten years, if that, as by then the Indians had
been pushed further up the Susquehanna and West on
the Potomac.

The later attacks, occurring from 1754 to 1760 by
the French in conjunction with the Indians, were made
at the foothills of the Blue Mountains, and old "Fort
Frederick" which was built by Governor Sharp in 1756,
at a cost of 6000 Pounds, was erected for defense at this
time.

Indians and bows and arrows, are almost synony-
mous. The Susquehannocks who met Captain John
Smith were equipped with these, as well as those who
greeted the Dove and Ark at St. Marys in 1634. It was
not long however, before the Indians lost their fear of
firearms and began to recognize the vast superiority
that firearms enjoyed over bows and arrows. Bows
and arrows of course always will have the great advantage of availability and silence; the latter, being a great
aid to a poor marksman. The Indians lost no oppor-
tunity in gaining possession of these, by fair means or
foul and though they never as a race became very
expert, they made up for this inferiority to the Whites,
by their skill in creeping close to their prey, which they
then could not fail to hit. To the South of Hudson Bay,
in 1740, when the bitter feud was in progress between
the Hudson Bay Company and the French who wished

to share the spoils but could not; the Indians were
deprived of ammunition for a time, as several of the
English ships carrying these supplies, were captured off
the coast. The Indians were in a destitute condition
and told the commandant at one of the forts, that they
had not used bows and arrows for a generation and that
they therefore had lost all skill in their use and begged
relief to prevent their starving to death. Anyone, with
a little practice, can become a passable shot with a
rifle, but only with a great deal of practice with a bow
and arrow can you be assured of meat.

Our Susquehannock Indians were in possession of
firearms, as Maryland actually supplied these Indians
with guns and barrels of powder and shot. The Iroquois obtained their guns, first from the Swedes and
Dutch and then from the English, who in 1664 had
captured New York, and these Indians were thus more
fully equipped to exterminate the Susquehannocks.
The Iroquois and Susquehannocks could not agree on
polity; the obvious remedy was for each if possible, to
exterminate the other. The remedy for differences of
this kind is so supremely simple, that we today, hesitate
to abandon such an old and tried institution. Simple
remedies being adapted to Indians and promptly put
into effect in this case, the Susquehannocks as a tribe
were annihilated within ten years and the Iroquois
themselves and by the same means, a few years later.
So much for ignorance and stupidity.

Indians and Settlement.—If reference is made to the
sketch of Lapidum, it will be noticed that the first
actual settler moved onto the land in the later part of
the sixteen nineties. Grants were taken out previous
to this, but no settlement occurred. On thinking along
these lines and wondering why the settlers were so
tardy in taking advantage of this choice spot, it oc-

curred to me that at least as late as 1680 there was a
village of Indians almost opposite Lapidum at the
mouth of the Octoraro Creek; there was another probably on the Island at the mouth of the Deer Creek, not
to speak of possible camps on Robert's and Wood's
Islands in the Susquehanna. No wonder the settlers
were slow in risking their livestock and families until
these villages had been abandoned. The fact that the
flats at the mouth of the Octoraro did support a thriving village in 1680 is well substantiated by testimony
of various persons made in 1734 and by the same
testimony, positive evidence of a Susquehannock fort
there as late as 1650 or 1660. These later Indians were
Shawnee, Nanticokes and Delawares. The settlers on
the Harford side if there were any, during the Indian
occupation of those village sites, would be aware at
night of the monotonous beat of the Tom Tom; faint
shouts and cries, the howling of half-starved dogs and
the glimmer of dozens of camp fires. It would require
a brave or foolhardy man to settle near Lapidum much
before 1700.

One of the witnesses called to give testimony in
regard to the State boundary dispute some time between 1734 and 1760 was Elizabeth Murphee, and from
her the following facts were recorded.

"Elizabeth Murphee says she knows Pensilvania and
some of the upper part of M'yl'd. That she knows the
River Susquehanna and that the same river thro
M'yl'd in Pen'lvania. That she has seen an old Indian
fort, that an Indian Town is open about it where they
plant, but an Indian fort is enclosed with wood stuck
in ye ground and earth thrown up to it. That she has
seen an old Indian fort upon Susquehanna River near
ye mouth of ye creek called Octoraro. That she be-
lieves ye same was an Indian fort because when she

ENTRANCE TO THE "LAND OF PROMISE"

went up with her father, Jonas Arskine, between thirty and forty years agoe to live at Octoraro among ye Indians of whom he had obtained leave. That her father lived there and in plowing up ye ground for corn there were banks of earth which they were obliged to levell. That her father who had traded long among ye Indians told her these were the banks of the Old Indian Fort. That ye old Indians who lived at ye same place often told her that was their fort, that there had been many battles fought there. That she had seen great numbers of dead mens bones in plowing up the ground there, and was told these were ye bones of the men who were killed there. That she never knew any other Indian fort." (Penn. Archives.)

Soapstone Bowls.—On a certain ridge located a mile or two North of Dublin, there is an outcrop of Soapstone or Steatite. On this ridge, before the leaves appear in the Spring, may be found numbers of Indian bowls and pieces of bowls, from one hundred pounds in weight down to those the size of an egg cup and on a certain part of this ridge is the quarry from which the Indians removed the stone. These bowls are all in an unfinished state, as it was easier for the workmen to chip off the heavier parts at the quarry, than to attempt to remove the whole chunk to their villages where it might be broken in manufacture, thus causing the Indians a back breaking journey for nothing. Indians up the Susquehanna used soapstone bowls to a very slight extent as the material is not found up there and the trade seemed to have been lacking.

Neither the Susquehannocks nor the Iroquois, made use of the large stone axe heads which are found now and then throughout the County. They were used by the Algonkin tribes who inhabited the country before the Susquehannocks had arrived and lived here also after the Susquehannocks had left. The axes were not very effective in chopping, but wonderfully efficient in smashing up firewood, those we find on our farms were no doubt lost long ago by squaws on wood foraging expeditions. The large clumsy flint arrowheads are of Algonkin make as well; the Susquehannocks using the triangular points, in common with the Iroquois. It is hard for a beginner to tell where one influence begins and where another leaves off, as the Susquehannocks and Algonkins adopted much from each other and to their mutual advantage.

Indian Shell Heaps in Harford County.—I am indebted to Mr. William B. Marye for the following information.

The Indians inhabiting the shores of the Bay during the seventeenth century and before, were in the habit of fishing for oysters in order to piece out their larders. The records which they have left of these feasts are in the form of shell heaps along the shore and now covered with soil. Oyster bars apparently existed further up the Bay in early times than they do today, the most northerly group of bars at present being situated half way between Poole's Island and the mouth of Worton Creek on the Eastern Shore. In the seventeenth century there existed an oyster bar to the East of the mouth of Bush River. It lies there at present; the shells old and full of holes are a constant source of annoyance to fishermen who snag their nets on the projections. These ancient shell-heaps are found on the banks and being exposed to erosion are easily visible to anyone walking along the water's edge. The Northernmost heap, appears to be situated on the North bank of Romney Creek, and is now owned by the Government and included in its reservation. There are seven or more on both banks of Bush River near the mouth and several on the East bank of the Gunpowder. I once excavated a small shell heap in New Jersey and obtained bones and teeth and pottery and also a long crude iron nail, which was possibly used in opening the oysters and then lost. The fact that brackish water which is required for oyster, does not reach as near the head of the Bay as formerly, can only be accounted for by the gradual silting up of the channel, thus preventing the tide from ascending as far as it did in those times.

There was little settlement along the river and above the Deer Creek prior to seventeen hundred. Even as late as 1799 Hauducoeur's map shows Rigbie, Worthington, Stump, Coale, and Hopkins as the only settlers. The region in 1700, must have been an almost unbroken wilderness. The ridge on which Darlington and Berkley stand, was undoubtedly covered with enormous white oaks, one grove blending into the next, with column like walnuts growing on sunny bottom lands and here and there through the forests, chestnuts of gigantic size. The silence of the woods at noon would be broken only by the intermittent rapping of the pileated woodpecker, or the distant sound of a solitary woodsman's axe; and if you paused to listen, the ever present roar of the old Susquehanna, which has been now unfortunately silenced.

Game.—Bear were plentiful and even as late as 1830 William Spence used to hunt wolves along the river. He lived in the lock house above the Paper mill. On January 1, 1816 a wolf was killed in West Nottingham and reported in Samuel N. Rhoad's book, "Mammals of Pennsylvania and New Jersey." In Rupp's "History of York and Lancaster Counties," it is stated that a wolf was seen crossing the ice from York County into Lancaster County and this in 1835. In 1798 in the new Court House in Bel Air, a bounty law was passed, legalizing payments in Harford County of thirty dollars a head for old wolves and four dollars apiece for young ones, besides eight cents each for crows.

New Roads.—About this time, there seems to have been a movement to improve and straighten roads, not only here, but in Cecil as well. The one that I have in mind in Cecil, is the road from "Mount Welcome Corner" to what was then known as Dorsey's Mill on the Conowingo Creek. Previous to this the road between these points was extremely crooked, passing on a long angle to the entrance to "Success Farm," now owned by Miss Goldie Smith; up this lane and thence behind the new church on the hill just above, then in front of the barn and old "Smiths Fort" on the next farm to the North and so on. In 1795 the road was surveyed and straightened as it is approximately today; at Oakwood, there is a short stretch however, which is now abandoned to woods. The road from Bel Air through Churchville to "Smith's Ferry" (Lapidum) was built in 1791 and a number of others; such as, from Peach Bottom to the state line and thence via Preston's Mill, on the Deer Creek, to Baltimore town and, "By the most convenient route." Another, from the "Bald Friar Ferry" to Bel Air.

But to get back to the settlement of the country. In the early decades of the eighteenth century, large tracts of land were purchased or otherwise obtained, by a few wealthy and influential men. These tracts of land were always recorded under some name more or less appropriate, such as "Brother's Discovery," "Maiden's Mount," "Phillip's Purchase," "Eight-rupp," (the derivation of this name will be probably found in Wales, England, as the original owner, Griffiths is a Welsh name). Others are "Dear Bought

Nothing Got," "Arabia Petrea," "Bachelor's Delight," "Conveniency," "Land of Promise," and so on. Clearings were made in the forest, probably by girdling the trees the year before, which prevented suckering and crops were in many cases planted for the first few seasons between the stumps. Slaves did the hard work. The trunks were rolled with the help of oxen and chains, into long windrows, where they were set on fire and in the early days the skies at night were seldom free from the glow of these fires. The whole operation was a most devastating piece of waste and folly. But it is easy to criticize our ancestors for ruthlessly cutting and destroying the forests, until we stop a moment and consider their situation when we are forced to admit that they may have had sufficient justification.

From the earliest dawn of intelligence in humanity and I go back, in all courtesy 75,000 years to the race of men called Neanderthals; man has had a dread of the dark, the wolves and the mystery of the forest, which always seems to be waiting and listening, but never doing. The Neanderthal man was extraordinary, in that he was able to domesticate fire. No man previous to this time could lay claim to having fire for his servant, as we find human bones in conjunction with charcoal 75,000 years ago in round numbers, but not before. These brutish looking men were afraid and were not backward in showing it. Every carnivorous animal was against him and the chances are that there were plenty. The man knew only too well that if he loitered in the cold and snow after dark on his return from a hunt, wolves would be soon slinking behind him, always a little nearer, the swift rush, a cry, and the sound of tearing and fighting. He squatted in a cave with his fire near him, looking out into the blackness. The forest supplied him with food to be sure, but it also hid the wolves.

Early man in England built enormous earthworks on hilltops. Here he lived and raised his herds of dwarf, shaggy cattle. All below were the woods, which couldn't be cut down and wouldn't burn and from which each night came the mournful cries of the ever watchful wolves. The cattle had to be watered of course, but rather than run the risk of driving them down into some ravine where they might be lost, the men constructed at a great expenditure of labor, what are called today "Dew Ponds"; these are situated on the hilltops, which were covered with close, green turf. The "dew ponds" were constructed as follows: An excavation was made and banks thrown up to enclose a space possibly of half an acre. All over the bottom and sides, a thick layer of straw was placed and on top of that, an equally thick layer of clay, completely covering and protecting the straw and its edges at the banks. The clay basin had to be watertight. It is a warm, clear night. The clay basin being insulated by the straw from the warm earth underneath, has cooled down enough to condense the moisture in the warm night air and of a consequence, heavy dew is deposited in the pond on the clay and this is added to night after night and as long as the clay blanket is not broken through. Sheep were not kept at this time, as their sharp feet were more likely to cut through into the straw and thus hopelessly ruin the dew pond. A few ponds are in working order today and look much like our ice ponds.

In America, in addition to the hostile animals, there were hostile Indians, one more incentive for pushing back the edge of the forest. This situation has happily passed, although the woodland owners in Harford

County have apparently overlooked the fact judging
from the frightful inroads of the portable saw mill on
our few remaining stands of timber.

Colonel Nathan Rigbie.—One of the most influential
settlers in Eastern Harford County in the early eighteenth century, was Colonel Nathan Rigbie and thanks
to the pen of Mr. Albert Silver, a short account of him
and his sons, has been preserved. Nathan was the son
of James Rigbie, who settled in Anne Arundel County
as an Indian Agent in the latter part of the seventeenth
century; here Nathan was born on April 28, 1695,
becoming an orphan at the age of five. On his majority,
he became a planter in that county, where he remained
until his grandfather, Thomas Tench willed him a tract
of land of two thousand acres on the Susquehanna
River, called "Phillip's Purchase." This tract, extended from near Shure's landing to Glen Cove; its
Western boundary passing through Darlington. Before removing to the new estate, Rigbie made several
sales, as funds were obviously low at this time. In
1728 Thomas Jones received one hundred acres. In
September of the same year, Gerrard Hopkins received
five hundred acres, and in 1731 two hundred acres
passed into the hands of Henry Coale. Rigbie retained
twelve hundred acres for himself and then settled in
1732 on his property, residing in the present residence
of Mr. Harold A. Jones. Here he lived the life of a
planter, growing quantities of tobacco, which he shipped
to England from Lapidum, leasing an acre of land there
in 1737 for that purpose. In addition to the culture of
tobacco, he operated a trading post and store, thus
supplying the needs of a community which sprang up
near him, forming the nucleus of Darlington. Many
people visited his store, as it was located on the "Upper
Route," extending from Joppa to the "Bald Friar

Ford." This store was evidently at his dwelling and
was patronized quite freely by friendly Indians, who
came to barter skins for powder, shot and kettles.
Having conducted the business for some time, he purchased two tracts of land, one at the mouth of the Deer
Creek called "Rigbies Hope," together with two
hundred and seventy-five acres of an adjoining tract,
known as "Parker's Chance" and on that part, recently occupied by Mr. John H. Price, were his slave
quarters, where he housed twenty-two slaves. A man
of the wealth and influence of Nathan Rigbie, could not
long remain in private life and he was chosen by Lord
Baltimore as one of the Justices of the Peace for Baltimore County, which of course included Harford at
that time. These justices, unlike those of today, besides guarding the peace, levied taxes as well, holding
regular meetings at Joppa. Esquire Rigbie now received the title of Lieutenant Colonel of the cavalry of
Baltimore County. This in August 1735. Baltimore
County included, besides Harford and Carroll, large
parts of Frederick and Howard Counties and the
cavalry or militia was in constant demand on the
various parts of this really large frontier in quelling
Indian uprisings against the settlers. Rigbie was also
a staunch backer of Lord Baltimore's claim for the
fortieth parallel and in conjunction with Thomas
Cresap, waged a ceaseless war against any encroach-
ment from Pennsylvania. At his house in Darlington,
were stored arms and supplies used in these forays and
on the property not far behind the house, was a building
of logs used as a prison for the captives, until they
could be transferred to safer accommodations at
Annapolis. In 1738 Colonel Rigbie was chosen High
Sheriff of Baltimore County, which office carried with
it dignity and importance second to none.

Farms in those days were comparatively innocent of fences and of a consequence, stock roamed more or less at will. It was therefore necessary for each owner to round up and mark his cattle and hogs every so often, that they might be distinguished from those of his neighbor and it was required that these marks be registered at the County Seat. On the Cassandra Coale plantation, a Crop and Slit in the left ear was used. At the home plantation, a Crop and Staple in each ear was made and at his slave quarters on the Deer Creek, a short Crop in each ear. Hogs were hunted in the woods and shot in the Fall when bacon was required. On September 29, 1737 Nathan Rigbie conveyed to the people called "Quakers" at Darlington, three and a half acres, for and in consideration of, twenty-eight Pounds. This is the property on which the Society of Friends has erected its meeting house and also includes the Oak Grove adjacent to it. It is said that the original meeting house stood in the Oak Grove. The Colonel was in his early days a member of this society, but was never a very strict observer of those principles, always caring more for worldly honor. His wife, Cassandra and children, joined the Deer Creek Presbyterian Church in 1740, he, himself, having been elected vestryman in St. George's Parish at Spesutia, in 1736.

Nathan and Cassandra were the parents of ten children, as follows: James, the eldest; Nathan, John, Thomas, Phillip, Skipworth, Elizabeth, Cassandra, Ann, and Susan.

James lived in the family residence at Darlington and was also, like his father, a prominent citizen. He was a captain of militia and was also High Sheriff of Baltimore County for the year, 1740. He married Elizabeth Harrison in 1741 and when she died, married Sarah Massey, the widow of Aquila Massey. Sarah

Massey probably lived in the house now owned by Mrs.
William Silver. He also had ten children. He joined
Friends and became a prominent minister of that society.
During Lafayette's march to Yorktown in 1781, Rigbie
entertained the marquis at his home, but did not long
survive the honor; departing this life in 1790 at the age
of seventy years.

Nathan Rigbie was one of the wealthiest men of his
time, as his personal property amounted to nearly
seven thousand dollars. He dressed with care, wearing
broadcloth and silk stockings, with silver shoe and knee
buckles and gold cuff buttons. His dwelling was
beautifully furnished with the usual silverware, books
and paintings. His wife Cassandra, dying in 1745
Rigbie married Sabina Rumsey of Cecil County and
died himself in 1752 at the age of fifty-seven years; his
remains rest in the graveyard at the Friends Meeting
in Darlington. After his father's death, the son James,
evidently had the boundary stones of "Phillip's Purchase" overhauled, as on one of these stones on the hill
near Glen Cove, is the inscription, "I. R. 1763."

CHAPTER III

Iron Furnaces and Forges

Forges and Furnaces.—The early settlers needed iron and plenty of it. Iron was expensive in England and buying it there was a cumbersome, inconvenient method. Therefore in 1719, by an act of the Assembly of Maryland, one hundred acres of land were offered to any one who would erect an iron furnace in Maryland and thus by 1756 there were eight furnaces and nine forges in the state; Principio Furnace in Cecil County, was the first, being erected in 1721.

Iron ore in Maryland is not very plentiful in any one spot, neither is it very rich and it is not strange that of the many furnaces that sprang up at this time, none should survive today. Bog ore or Limonite is seen in rough, yellowish slabs two or three inches thick, occurring in layers in banks in the neighborhood of the bay. This section was once under water and when in a boggy or swampy condition, was teeming with bacteria having the power to absorb soluble iron from the water and to precipitate it in an insoluble form. In due time these precipitations grew to several inches in thickness and were sometimes used by the early iron workers as a partial source of iron. Limonite, when ground to powder, incidentally makes the yellow ochre used in paint.

The lower Deer Creek had the amazing number of seven furnaces and forges between Stafford and the bridge on which U. S. 1 crosses the creek, a distance on the creek of about ten miles. The first was known as the "Rock Forge," built by George Rock about 1749 at Stafford. The next above, was "Cumberland Forge" at the upper edge of the Smith property. Then came "Lancaster Forge" or furnace one quarter of a mile above Priests Ford Bridge. Then further up, on the site of Miss Hannah Husband's flint mill, stood the "Nottingham Forge"; beyond this again, and three-quarters of a mile below the concrete bridge on U. S. 1, stood the "Lebanon Forge," which after a time, was replaced by "The Deer Creek Iron Works" operating as late as 1878, the remains of which, including those of a grist mill, owned by Moore & Company may be seen to-day immediately below the site of the Forge Bridge, which was swept out in a flood in January 1933. Near this site again, was the "Red Drum Forge." Surely this is an unsurpassed record of optimism or poor judgment, for the iron ore, always of a poor grade, occurred only in pockets along the hilltops, which, coupled with the speedy depletion of the forest resources, caused these primitive furnaces, one after another to be abandoned.

A Furnace and a Forge were and are, two entirely different things. Some of the aforementioned iron works were forges and some probably both.

Iron Furnaces.—An "Iron Furnace" is a large hollow truncated pyramid of stone, lined at the bottom with fire clay or brick. Into the lower part of the furnace, through pipes or "tuyers," blasts of air were admitted from huge bellows, working alternately by means of cranks and a water wheel. A fire was kindled by the operator inside and heavy pieces of wood thrown on little by little, until a roaring conflagration was started; then a load of iron ore was shot in from wheelbarrows, which were trundled out on a runway from a nearby bank to the top of the furnace. Next a load of charcoal, then oyster shell or lime, which acted as a flux, uniting the dirt and impurities into a slag, which floated off

from the molten metal; then more ore and more charcoal. The blast was then started and the creaking and
groaning of the bellows and the roaring of the flames
pouring from the top, particularly at night, was something long to remember. These furnaces produced
molten iron, which was finally run out into molds in the
earth before the furnace; a number of the molds were
usually connected to one channel, like a sow and her
pigs at meal time. Thus the derivation of the word
"Pig Iron."

Iron Forges.—A "Forge," on the other hand, de-
pended in the early days on pig iron from some other
source, scrap iron being used at present. A long wooden
building covered one or more puddling furnaces.
These were cast iron or brick affairs, like large chunk
stoves, with an opening and hearth in front of each.
Two "Tuyers" were inserted, one on each side, connecting with the interior. These tuyers were often
water cooled to minimize the intense heat. A fire of
charcoal was kindled in the furnace and when well
started, was blown white hot by the blast of air. Several
pigs of irons six feet long and six inches wide were now
pushed into the furnace and as the ends melted, they
were shoved in again and again. The metal, owing to
the reduction of the carbon by the blast, lay in the fire-
pot in a sticky viscid mass. The workmen now took
heavy levers and hooks and after prying the mass free
at the back, rolled it out onto the hearth with the hooks.
A crane and tongs caught the dazzling metal and bore
it along to a trip hammer located at one end of the
shed, where the "Bloom" of Iron was squashed out
into bars of uniform size, to be worked up later in
another process. This method produced wrought iron
such as blacksmiths use and of very different consist-

ency from the Pigs, which have but low tensile strength
and are only used in making castings.

The Trip Hammers used in these "Bloomeries" had
heads weighing several hundred pounds on the ends of
oak timbers twelve to fifteen feet long. They were
usually set parallel to the shaft of the water wheel and
wood spuds on this, lifted the hammer and let it fall
time after time as the water wheel shaft revolved. The
hammer had to be ponderously braced with timbers
and the anvil placed on deep foundations, as the jar
was exceedingly heavy.

Charcoal Burning.—Coal and coke were unknown in
those days, the obvious fuel being therefore charcoal
and it required an immense amount of it. One furnace
used 840 bushels every twenty-four hours, in producing
two tons of pig iron. The equivalent of this amount of
charcoal is about twenty-two cords of wood. In a
year's run, an ordinary furnace consumed in round
numbers, two hundred and forty acres of forest! Pits
disclose themselves today in a harrowed field, by the
dark color of the earth on a spot, possibly twenty feet
across. Cord wood of oak or hickory is cut, and when
seasoned, is stacked up on end around a central chimney, large enough to get down into. This stacking is
continued around and around and often a second tier
is placed on the first. When all is finished, sod and
damp leaves are placed all over the wood and earth is
shoveled over and around the pile, all but the central
chimney opening. A fire is then kindled at the bottom
of this flue and when well started, the operator takes a
crow bar and punches holes breast high all around and
through the earth into the interior for ventilation and
chips of wood are used to cover those not required
during any particular direction of wind. The charring
process takes from three to ten days and the "Coal

burner" has to be on hand day and night, in order to
stifle any sign of flame at the openings. I used to visit
these coal burners in the New Jersey pines, near Berlin.
In traveling across country, you first become conscious
of a thin acrid smell of creosote and on following up this
clue, you will find just such an earth covered mound,
and near it an earth covered hut, with a sloping door
set in the letter "A" gable end. The lonely chopper
is not far off and at night, the mournful barking of his
dog blends in the distance with the equally mournful
hooting of the great horned owl. To visit one of these
"Burners" is a most primitive experience. There are
none left now in New Jersey and but one or two in
Delaware. The reader has thus a general idea of early
iron manufacture in Harford County.

"The Cumberland Forge" was situated on the North
bank of the Deer Creek, one half mile above the mouth
of Elbow Branch. The lane leading up from it, is in a
deep hollow, and crosses the Smith's orchard lane
about halfway into the house. Remains of the forge
can be seen today among the weeds on the flat below.
This forge was built in 1749 by Nathan Rigbie, in conjunction with John Hall, Jacob Giles and Nathan
Rigbie Junior. The latter was manager for many
years. The deed from Jemima Forwood to the company, reads "to John Hall and Company in Iron
Works." In 1775 it was conveyed to Jacob Giles, Jr.
and in 1794 to John Stump. "Cumberland Forge"
obtained its pig iron by ship from some other point. It
was unloaded at Lapidum and conveyed by ox teams up
the hill past Dr. Virdin's dwelling, thus the origin of
"Pig Hill," then probably down Elbow branch to the
ford at Stafford and up across the Smith's orchard and
down again to the Cumberland Forge.

Little is known of these early forges and today even

their location is uncertain. However, in the ledger of
Thomas Archer for the year 1795, is recorded the fact
that he supplied many cords of wood to "Lancaster
Forge," which was located near Priests ford according
to the assessment books of 1764. This forge was sold
in 1760 to Corbin Lee at Nottingham Forge, and Archer
ceased hauling to Lancaster and hauled to Nottingham
instead.

These forges produced bar iron, which sold in 1740,
at about 30 English pounds a ton. In our currency this
is at the rate of seven and one-half cents per pound of
metal.

Rock Forge.—In 1749, a man named George Rock,
built or began building a forge at Stafford. Stephen
Onion, who had been manager at Principio Furnace in
1721, bought out his interest and organized a company known as the "Onion and Lawson Company."
The site of this forge is directly below the Smith house,
which was built by John Stump during his absence in
Europe in 1779. The heavy masonry with the road
along the bank above it, would be ideal for such a
furnace and the scattered lumps of slag about the site,
definitely indicate an iron furnace or forge. The forge
of "John Hall and Company" was operating at the
same time, a mile or more up the Creek.

ROCK RUN GRIST MILL

CHAPTER IV

GRIST MILLS AND OTHER MILLS

Grist Mills were essential to the early settlers. They sprang up almost automatically on all the streams capable of furnishing the necessary power. One of the earliest of these, as mentioned before, was built by Reuben Perkins at Lapidum, in the year 1760.

Rock Run Mill.—Nathaniel Giles built a grist mill here previous to 1760. It was probably not the present stone mill, but stood I believe, almost a half mile above the present mill dam and above the sharp turn in the road. The excavation may be seen today. The race is easily visible from the road and extends above, as far as the wooden bridge, where was situated the dam. The site lies on the property of Mr. J. G. D. Paul. The ruins of the mill face a beautiful bank of laurel and some of the stonework may still be seen. That Giles was the owner of this seat cannot be proved by actual evidence, but the probabilities are all in its favor. The Parker family, however, has no knowledge of having owned any such mill.

Returning now to the river. The present Rock Run mill was believed to have been built by John Stump in 1794, and was run in conjunction with the one at Stafford. About 1800 John Carter conducted business here in partnership with Stump and in 1804 built the dwelling above on the proceeds, but shortly after died. His wife now falling into financial difficulties was forced by Stump to abandon the property and if it is possible to flee in an ox cart, she fled to Frankford, Pennsylvania with her children. C. R. Smith, the miller, put his name on the cornerstone in 1841, having been miller at Wilson's Mill in 1837. The Archer family now appears. Henry W. Archer, a lawyer, fitted up the second story of the spring house above the mill, as an office, where he conducted his business. Joseph C. Parker was miller and for many years the firm name being, "Parker and Archer." From 1900 to 1928 John M. Macklen owned the mill and from then on to the present writing, Mr. W. W. Wilkinson, through no fault of his own conducts a dwindling trade. The overshot wheel is of iron and is approximately thirty-three feet in diameter.

Stafford Grist Mill.—In addition to his mill at Rock Run, John Stump also owned one at Stafford, which stood on the site of the present flint mill. The canal for these mills, had its source in a dam, which extended across the Deer Creek just above the mouth of Elbow branch. Part of it is still standing. The mill ground practically all the wheat produced in the neighborhood and continued to run into the 1880's, when my father who visited it then as a young man, reports that he found the miller busy grinding carloads of buffalo horns for the manufacture of yellow Pruciate of Potash. This was sold and shipped to Carter and Scattergood of Philadelphia.

In 1872 there were a million and a half buffalo shot in the West. In 1873 as many more, but in 1874 the total had suddenly dropped to 158,000 animals, or to one fifteenth of the previous slaughter. Thus and then was the bison exterminated. Ten years later as I have said, their bones were being ground in Maryland. There was one such spot at Frenchtown across the river and one certainly at Stafford.

In the early eighties and during the death struggles of the old mill, Edward M. Allen, Senior, owned and operated it. Bones as well as horns were ground here

and even some of the children in the neighborhood
used to collect them and sell them to Mr. Allen. One
particular cow's skull elicited the remark, that he had
paid for it six times already. The present flint mill,
was built on its site and at about this time. There was
also a wagon shop here and a cannery, which Mr. Ned
Allen operated.

Bark Mill.—A quarter of a mile above the flint mill
and at the far end of the row of stone dwellings now in
ruins, stood in 1845, the tanbark mill of Gideon Smith.
It stood on the site of the "Rock Forge," below the
Charles Smith house. Black Oak, contains a large
amount of tannin, which as might be imagined is the
active principle in the process of tanning leather. The
oak trees were cut about corn planting time when the
bark would slip off easily. It was then removed and
leaned on edge against the logs to dry out while the logs
were sawed up for firewood. The bark was now hauled
to the mill, where it was weighed on enormous steel-
yards so that the man might be paid his due wages. The
bark was next broken in small pieces and thrown into
a hopper and a horse usually did the remainder by
grinding it into a fine powder, filling the cart underneath and the air above with a quantity of choking dust
which settled in your hair, eyes and ears. Gideon
Smith lived here and operated the mill, later removing
to Glen Cove.

At the time of the "Cumberland Forge" in 1749,
which was built by Nathan Rigbie, there was a ford
across the Deer Creek at Stafford, but no bridge.
Neither did the road from Darlington follow its present
course. At Reid Jourdan's dwelling, it followed Charles
Smith's orchard lane until it joined the Cumberland
Forge road crossing the ridge near where the recent
apple shed used to stand. It then turned into this

road and emerged on the present Stafford road in a kind of gully, just two-tenths of a mile from the end of the iron bridge. Traces of stone buildings are visible along this old lane and flotillas of Day Lilies, indicate the door yards of many houses long since gone. As late as 1870 or 1880 there was a wooden covered bridge over the Deer Creek at Stafford. There is no photograph of this bridge extant, but there occurred here a rather curious incident. A colored woman now dead, named Sabina Johnson, having been with some companions on a midnight frolic in the neighborhood, was returning via this covered bridge. About half way through, their merriment was changed to terror, when in the pitch darkness they stumbled over some cows lying on the floor. An iron bridge succeeded to the wooden one and when this was washed out, the present bridge was built. It was erected in 1904. There was also a wooden covered bridge over the mouth of Rock Run at the same time and was no doubt, replaced at the same time. I have a photograph in which it is shown.

In 1812 while "John Stump of Stafford" owned the aforementioned grist mill, flour was sold by him to the British; his rule being to charge as much silver for a barrel of flour as would lie edge to edge on the head of the barrel. This business acumen, did not excuse him if true from being a traitor. He was born in 1752 and died in 1816, four years after this episode.

Stafford Flint Mill.—This mill was recently set on fire by some of our citizens for the scrap iron contained in the upper parts, with the result that it is almost completely demolished. The mill was built about 1880 by Thomas Symington for the purpose of grinding soapstone, but B. Gilpin and Joshua C. Smith, put it to use in grinding flint. The flint arrived on canal boats from their quarry near Bald Hill and unloaded at the mill docks on the Deer Creek. The canal at that time, extended across the mouth of the creek, damming it so that canal boats were enabled to ascend to the present bridge. A spillway immediately below the mouth of the creek, allowed flood water to escape into the river from the canal and the tow path crossed this spillway on a rickety arched wooden bridge, which disappeared during the nineties. Francis Stokes and his brother Joseph when young men, while walking up the tow path from Lapidum about 1850, saw, lodged in one of these spillways, two slaves chained together by their wrists and drowned, having attempted no doubt to escape from their master. About 1880 the Smith brothers operated a flint mill on the river a mile or so above the Deer Creek, but becoming interested in paper manufacture, they relinquished their interest at Stafford and Horace Stokes took it over. In its heyday, this section of the creek had a different aspect than it has today. The hill behind the plant was bare of trees. A path of stones with planks thereon, enabled the men to cross the stream, as the bridge was evidently out of commission at this particular time. Large sheds and warehouses covered perhaps two acres of ground contiguous to the present stone building, with quiet deep water up to the mill docks. In one of these sheds, there was a boiler, which heated the pipes used in drying out the flint sludge.

Samuel and Randal Wallis' Mill.—The next grist mill on the Deer Creek, stood and still stands on the north bank, about a mile and a half above Stafford. The ruins are all overgrown with vines, but the stonework is still in beautiful condition. This mill was known as "The Samuel and Randal Wallis' Mill," but was never put in operation, as the builders had not reckoned on John Stump of Stafford. Stump, fearing their competition,

bought in all the wheat at a high price, thus forcing
The Wallises who could not meet it, to abandon their
expensive project. The finish of the War of 1812 and
the consequent slump in prices, may also have been a
big factor.

Wilson's Mill.—A mile or two above the Wallis seat,
stands the mill recently bought by Mr. F. J. Stokes and
known as Wilson's Mill. Its early history is nebulous,
as the information given in the deeds is scanty and often
apparently conflicting. There is no mention however
of a mill or dam previous to 1743.

The mill is located on the Western End of a tract of
land known as "Parker's Chance," which was patented
to George Parker by the Proprietor in 1684. He deeded
it in turn to Nathan Rigbie, Jr., the second son of
Colonel Nathan Rigbie in 1743, who retained it until
his death in 1783. Rigbie's will states that he be-
queaths his mill and dam, so the probabilities are that
he built Wilson's Mill. One point that befogs the issue
is the fact that a man named John Austin who arrived
from England at Baltimore in May 1795, owned land
contiguous to this mill seat and as is said, settled on the
Deer Creek near Darlington, erecting a house and a
grist mill there, which was called Austin's Mill. His
son, John, while repairing the mill which was damaged
by a flood, caught cold and died of pneumonia in 1807.
Probably Rigbie built the original mill and Austin rebuilt or repaired it, who can tell. In 1802, the property
was deeded to Joseph Brinton and in 1821 to Reuben
Stump and in 1856 to Rachel Price; her second husband
being William Wilson. Their child David E. Wilson
was born here in 1822 and his Uncle C. R. Smith,
operated the mill in 1837 as miller during the ownership
of Reuben Stump. David inherited the property from
his mother in 1866 and his son D. Gilpin Wilson ob-

Wilson's Mill Bridge over the Deer Creek

tained it by deed in 1903 and operated it until September 1931, when it was bought by Francis J. Stokes. The mill has at present a ten foot six inch fall from the dam and develops twenty-five horsepower. In the stone work on the front of the mill, are carved these inscriptions:

S. B. Silver 1817

E. R. 1822

C. R. Smith 1837.

The original mill house was of logs and stood above the spring and beech tree. Perhaps this was the house built by John Austin. On a cold winter night in 1856, it caught fire and burned to the ground and the present stone dwelling of Mr. Stokes was built shortly after by David E. Wilson. The public road from Harmony Church to Darlington used to cross the Deer Creek on a covered bridge directly opposite the little stone miller's house. This bridge was washed out in a freshet in 1865 and the covered bridge which was built three years later further down the creek, suffered the same fate in 1931. (See Illustration.)

Deerdale Mill.—This mill was probably located on the north side of the Deer Creek, on the present property of Mr. Oscar Duncan. There are still traces of the race and also of the dam, which was a small one and was located near the mouth of the stream flowing around the base of Mountain Hill. There was no mill seat near Death's ford on the Deer Creek.

Nobles Mill.—William Noble operates the next grist mill on the Creek. It was built by Gerard Gover in 1854, the timbers having been sawed out on his pit saw above the mill, traces of which are still to be seen. The long floor joists are forty feet long and were too long for the saw carriage to handle and hence had to be hewn

with a broad axe and afterward planed. Mr. Noble
says the grist mill was in operation when his father took
it over in 1860 and as a boy he often helped in the saw
mill. He said that the shock and jar of the pit saw was
terrific and it was only possible to edge boards by
laying them on logs and sawing through both together.
The new concrete dam was built in 1921. In the flood
of 1933, the water rose in the mill to six feet seven
inches over the first floor and deposited eight inches of
mud there. Wm. Noble was upstairs at the time and
was forced to remain there overnight and until the
waters subsided. He failed to mention the dove. The
freshet washed away all his saw logs and flooded over
the iron bridge burying it a yard deep in trash, which
had all to be removed before a single team could cross.
Above the remains of the pit saw, are traces of another
old mill of which Mr. Noble knows nothing. This mill
seat according to Mr. Frederick Williams, belonged in
1779 to John Hawkins, who without a doubt had some
kind of a mill on this spot. Mr. Noble, showed me his
father's account books, containing feed accounts of the
Woolseys, Silvers, S. A. Williams and many others.
These accounts ran as high as nine hundred dollars a
year. The farmers regularly made five trips a week.
They brought corn to be ground for their cattle and
hauled back the ground meal at an average of sixteen
dollars a load. The mill had to run day and night in
shifts, to keep up with the business. These farmers he
said, were much better pay than those of our time.

The Glasgow Mill.—The site of this mill is one hundred and fifty yards below the present pike at Priest's
Ford bridge and on the South side of the road. It was
thought to have been built by the Jesuit priests about
1750, for use at their Chapel on the hill above. In
1814, it was bought by Dr. James Glasgow, who never

operated it himself, the name thus having no real significance. Some crumbling walls remain, two small
millstones and traces of the old race, but little else.
There is more on the same subject under the Priests
Ford Monastery.

Bennett's Mill.—Finally we have William Bennett's
mill. This stood at the mouth of Thomas's Run; the
mill seat being taken up by him in 1749. There were
twenty acres and, as the records state, was near
"Johnson's Ford."

Flint Mills.—There are few sections of the country
as well supplied with white flint as the Eastern part of
Harford County and flint grinding, though not as
primitive an industry in this country as the smelting of
iron or of the manufacture of flour, is fully as interesting
a process. In order that the reader may not be unduly
bored with the following account of flint grinding I will
be as brief as possible. Ground flint makes a most
excellent material for the manufacture of china, but in
order to obtain this material, a rather complicated
process must be followed, which is as follows:

The white flint is quarried from the bank and the
impure colored parts are discarded. The pure flint is
now hauled to the mill, either in canal boats as at the
Stafford Mill, or by wagons, as was the case at the
Conowingo Flint Mill. The lime kiln where the trans-
formation begins, is a squatty chimney-like affair built
of stone usually against a bank, with an opening at the
bottom and one at or near the top and having a con-
stricted waist. Across the waist inside a grate of cord
wood is placed and then chunks of flint are thrown on.
Cord wood is uniformly mixed with the flint until the
kiln is as full as possible. A fire is now started under
the grate perhaps at four o'clock in the afternoon and
the whole mass of wood takes fire and heats the flint

intensely hot. The kiln will burn out during the night
and in the morning the contents will have fallen through
the charred grate onto the ground. It is now in a
crumbly condition and may easily be shoveled out and
the impure parts which have turned dark in the burning, are separated out and the remainder is ready for
the next step. This is crushed to a uniform size and
placed in a large circular hopper six feet or so in diameter and two large circular granite mill stones on edge,
called "Chasers" roll round and around on one hori-
zontal spindle in a sort of elephantine race, crushing
the coarser particles to a fine powder in their passage.
A conveyor constantly removes the coarser powder
forced to the periphery of the race track and returns it
to the center to be reground. After the flint has been
ground down to a uniform fineness, it is shoveled into
a so-called "Pan." This is another circular hopper,
four feet larger in diameter than the other, watertight
and having a bottom formed of smooth flint stones.
In this, by means of large oak cross beams which are
revolved from above, heavy flint stones with flat faces
are slid round and around on the bottom, each stone
pushed by one end of the crossed timbers. Water is
admitted and the powder with the water finally becomes a fine smooth paste. The grinding goes on day
and night. After a suitable length of time, this paste
of ground flint is run out onto steam pipes which lie on
the floor and the heat slowly dries the material to
powder. The test used is to pass the powder through
a wire mesh of two hundred wires to the inch. The
finished material found its way, at least from the
Conowingo mill, to the various pottery works at
Trenton New Jersey, where much china and porcelain
is manufactured.

There were a number of these Flint Mills in the

Eastern part of the county and they were situated on streams large enough to furnish the necessary power, (it took plenty of it) and contiguous to an outcrop of flint. The Smith brothers had one at Stafford and another near the site of the paper mill and later another at Conowingo, utilizing the same machinery.

"The Trenton Flint and Spar Company."—This mill burnt flint on Broad Creek, about a half mile above the present shoreline of the lake. When the water is quiet and you know just where to look, you can see the top of one of the kilns several feet under the surface of the lake. This Company also owned the flint kiln at Stafford which stands closest to the public road. They were fortunate in being located above the feeder dam at Broad Creek.

When the canal was in operation the opening and closing of the locks took an immense amount of water, the compensation being obtained from creeks like Deer Creek and Broad Creek. This was obtained from Deer Creek by a method already described, but the canal at Broad Creek, being higher above the mouth of the stream, a dam on this stream was necessary to flood the water up to the height of the canal. The dam was built across Broad Creek a short distance below the Trenton Spar Company's kilns and a race from this, on the north side, conducted the "feeder" water into the canal, which latter, passed over the mouth of the creek on an aqueduct. The company built a warehouse near this aqueduct and between the creek and the race. I remember seeing the foundation of it. It is quite obvious that the Spar Company could load its boats at its docks and float them through the race past the warehouse and into the canal. The Company's own power dam was located of course above the mill, but now impossible to locate. This Company went the way of all flesh in the 1890's. Above the old "Red Bridge," which was wooden and covered in all modesty and since replaced by the modern concrete colossus, stood the

Flint Mill of H. Clay Whiteford.—This mill continued to grind until about 1922, when the funds ran low and it was shut down. I have gone through it often and I believe the kilns were made of brick. The Whiteford Mill obtained its flint from its own quarry on top the hill on the South side of the Creek and also from the flint quarry below Bald Hill. The road used in hauling this led out of the quarry and up through the woods on Bald Hill and then straight down the ravine to the wooden bridge, which now spans one arm of the lake. There is said to have been a small amount of gold found in the flint from this quarry and a number of people have panned for it in the stream above Bald Hill. We will leave for a time this fascinating region of greenbrier and hairbells and transport ourselves now to the Deer Creek.

Husband's Mill.—A half mile below the bridge formerly used by the pike in crossing this stream, stood the flint mill of Miss Hannah Husband, known as "Husband's Mill." I suspect it occupied the approximate site of the "Nottingham Forge." The flint being obtained from outcrops on the hill above. This plant operated until about 1920. A dozen worn out "Chasers" may be seen taking their ease in the bushes today; a broken dam, crumbling kilns and prostrate timbers are all that is left of a once thriving industry. The eighteen or twenty head of mules used at the plant, were housed in the barn of Miss Husband on the top of the hill, but were unfortunately burnt to death, during an incendiary fire one night as it was impossible to get them loose. At one time a vagrant was employed at the mill. He had been bled shortly before, at a hospital for some trouble or other and rather enjoying the sensation, had made a habit of climbing the hill behind the kilns and bleeding himself. This habit was practiced rather extensively also by Indian squaws and for the same reason. At all events the man one day failed to make his appearance; a search was instituted and he was discovered having by accident or design bled himself to death.

The Conowingo Flint Mill, operated by B. G. Smith, resembled the others in most particulars, which will not be necessary to repeat. Who owned it after the Smiths sold it, I do not know. At any rate, in 1920 it was operated by Mr. Ned Allen and James Wilson and known as the "Indian Rock Flint Company." Mr. Charles A. Swift was their manager and kindly gave me the following information. The flint came from the Castleton quarry, where the partners owned one hundred and forty-eight acres including Bald Hill. The flint was quarried by the Presberry boys (colored) and hauled by mule team across the old Conowingo bridge to the flint mill. The Knights did some of this hauling and I can well remember meeting these wagons driven with one line and six head of mules on the narrow dirt road between Glen Cove and the bridge. The driver invariably took the edge side and let the buggies keep to the bank. I also well remember at Darlington, hearing in the dead of night the ceaseless grinding of the machinery at Conowingo. Personally I prefer it to the noise of the automobiles; but that cannot be helped now.

Some of the flint hauled to this mill was burnt and ground and some was merely crushed and not burnt. The latter, was shipped in graded sizes to the Grasseli Chemical Company in Cleveland, Ohio, where it was used in filtering a certain kind of liquid gas. The mill

received eight dollars a ton for this. The business did
not make any progress as surplus funds instead of being
saved were immediately dissipated, till finally the
property was leased to the "Conowingo Stone and
Stucco Company" of Philadelphia. This new company
now began to earn money and took in thousands of
dollars a month on stucco stone or coarse grit. The
flint could be obtained at the quarry in various shades.
Mr. Swift built a new dam below the railroad bridge
and dug his race from one corner of it, but unfortunately
the Philadelphia Electric Company drowned them out
in 1927, thus ushering in a new era for better or for
worse.

Lime Kilns.—Although York County has so much
limestone, Harford County has little or none, although
it was burnt by individuals here and there. One such
lime kiln stood on the West bank of the canal, at what
was then known as "Sedgie's Landing," which termi-
nated the road leading down through the Castleton
quarry. This kiln was built by Hugh Jones and was
used for burning lime to be spread later on his own
fields; the limestone arrived from York County on
canal boats at this dock. Since the abandonment of
this cheap form of transportation, it is more profitable
to ship the burnt lime, the loss in weight thus offsetting
the cost of burning. The process of burning limestone
is practically identical with that of flint which I need
not repeat.

There lived in Darlington in the early years of the
nineteenth Century, a man by the name of R. I. Jackson. His dwelling was the beautiful stone house now
owned by Mr. George W. Robinson on the Stafford
road. Jackson was born in 1810 and about the time of
the Civil War conducted a mercantile business both at
Darlington and at Glen Cove. He built at Glen Cove,

a battery of four lime kilns, three of large diameter and the other smaller and burnt lime regularly here as did his successors for years; the product being sold locally to the farmers. He also built warehouses and a store as well, along the canal and north of "Peddlers Run." These buildings stood close to the road, the latter entering here a kind of canyon white with lime dust and redolent of bone meal. I remember it distinctly but of course years later. At Darlington opposite his home and in the present dwelling of Mr. Samuel C. Bishop, he stored certain kinds of merchandise such as blacksmith iron, nails and bone meal. The building was at that time covered with vertical boards like a barn and the second floor rooms only were plastered. He had one pair of horses, a carriage and buggy, and evidently paid for heavy hauling. Mr. Jackson had no children. In his later years, he wore a long white beard up to his eyes. His picture gives the impression of a man at least one hundred and fifty years old, but he died in 1872 at the puerile age of sixty-two. He was survived by his widow who sold both buildings and the farm in 1896 to Alfred Edge, the latter selling it two years later to Mr. Robinson.

R. I. Jackson kept slaves as was the custom here before the Civil War. During the occupancy of Alfred Edge, certain repairs were necessary at the rear part of the second floor. On hammering here a hollow reverberation was heard and on removing the plaster, a door was disclosed barred with iron, closing the entrance to a room behind it. Here they kept some of the slaves. On investigation, I discovered an old colored woman, whose sister now dead, with some others, was regularly locked up in this room by Mrs. Jackson each night. She said her sister was born a slave here and one day she did something which displeased Mrs. Jackson,

who picked up a butcher knife and slashed her across
the back of the hand, these scars remained with her till
her dying day. I have been told this tale from both
sides and there can be little doubt of its truth. The
warehouses at Glen Cove fell into the hands of Dr.
Robert Archer after Jackson's death and in 1882 he
sold out to "Barnes and Archer," who conducted a
mercantile business here for four years. Mr. B. H.
Barnes, a brother of the above and who gave me this
information, did clerk work for the firm. In 1886 the
partnership of "Smith and Allen,"* took over the
business and ran it until bought out by a man named
Emlen, and he in turn by Charles A. Andrew. The
latter assisted by James Jones sold supplies here for
some years. Their whitewashed office stood on the
top of one of the abandoned lime kilns and was known
locally as the "Castle," but about 1911 the new pike
was put through and in order to obtain the necessary
width, the warehouses were torn down and Mr. Andrew
moved to Conowingo.

Paper Mill.—When we glance back over the last one
hundred and fifty years of industrial life, we are im-
pressed by the amazing number of failures. Perhaps
the very elements which lend this county its charm, are
not the ones necessary for sustaining business. Our
county has undoubted charm, as is proved by the
constant increase in the alien population and if Emerson
is correct when he states in his "Rhodora," that beauty
is its own excuse for Being, then perhaps we should let
industry go by the board and be thankful that we live
in such a beautiful county.

One industry now gone, which spells Romance for
many of us who live near the river, was that of paper
manufacture. "The Susquehanna Power & Paper

* Cortauld W. Smith, Edw. M. Allen, Sr.

Company" had its birth in the fertile brains of Joshua
C. and B. Gilpin Smith. These brothers had, in 1880,
a flint mill on the river, but becoming interested in the
manufacture of paper and knowing nothing about it
themselves, persuaded Harry Carter who lived in
Cecil County on the Elk River, to teach them the
business and to act as manager of a mill which they
proposed building and organizing. Carter accepted,
stockholders were rounded up, and the mill was begun.
The spot selected was just below the site of their flint
mill and on a flat piece of land opposite Amos' Island
and about a mile above the present dam. A wing dam
was built out in the river almost up to Glen Cove,
which conducted the water to the headgates. There
was only an eleven or twelve foot head of water and
the turbines had to be large in diameter and were few
in number. The grindstones were attached to the
turbines and used an enormous amount of power in
grinding the wood. This was bought and shipped from
Nova Scotia. The canal ran past the mill with convenient docks for unloading supplies. It was crossed
by a wooden plank bridge at the mill, which was used
by teams and pedestrians. Below the mill a quarter of
a mile, was the settling pond from which clean water
was secured for washing the pulp when the river was
muddy, and we boys used to haunt its shores in attempting to shoot the huge "snappers" that lived
there. The "Ground wood" process was used here, as
well as the "Sulphite." There was always a strong
sulphurous smell at the mill and in front, were often
large piles of yellow sulphur and barrels of rosin, the
latter for sizing the paper. Canal boats often tied up
at the dock with loads of coal, or passed down the canal,
the steersman nonchalantly leaning back on the sweep
smoking his pipe and saluting some "buddy" on the

dock. It was a fascinating spot for a boy. The first order for paper was from the "New York American," a pink journal at six cents a pound. This was a very high price and the company made lots of money. In 1889, the year of the Johnstown Flood, the canal, the artery of the mill, was partially washed out and canal boats were stuck in the mud from one end to the other. A hundred men were employed in repairing a break just below the Conowingo bridge. In the next year there was another flood, which so discouraged the stockholders of the Canal Company that it was abandoned. Money was now borrowed to build an overhead conveyor from the railroad across the river, which was done at great expense. An endless cable traveled over and back carrying buckets for coal and slat baskets for pulp. The cable sagged down in the middle of the river and at high water sometimes got caught and daredevils frequently went out to free it. On one of these attempts, three men went out and were washed off and drowned, and the body of one of them was found a month later near Port Deposit, tethered by a string to a root. Competition from other mills now began in earnest and the price for paper finally dropped to two cents. Here profit nearly or completely ceased. This was the turning point in the mill's career, but it struggled on until 1901, when, having lost a great deal of money for its stockholders it was finally abandoned.

"Old Forge Bridge" over the Deer Creek

CHAPTER V

Unrelated Sketches

The Gover Seminary.—A fascinating legend has lingered for many years about a small heap of stones on the hilltop overlooking Rock Run, but like a fragrant perfume, it vanishes when you attempt an analysis. During the first quarter of the nineteenth century, there lived about a mile back from the Susquehanna River above Rock Run, four sisters, Margaret, Susan, Hannah and Caroline Gover. Their home was large, with circular stone steps in front and surrounded by brick walks bordered with shrubbery. The view from the front was a commanding one as it is today, overlooking the broad expanse of the river with its many islands and gleaming rapids. It also overlooked the covered bridge which crossed the river at Rock Run at that time. In the neighborhood, several wealthy families resided on their farms and here and there an Indian lived in quiet seclusion in the woods. In such a paradise, the mind if freed from drudgery, gradually becomes like a precious stone in a beautiful setting and the sisters answering the demand made upon them, determined to invite their friends and all those young ladies of the neighborhood who valued their spiritual and mental qualities, to meet at their home and to aid in forming a school to be known as "The Gover Seminary." There appeared to be no lack of pupils both day scholars and boarders; the neighbors often furnishing lodging for the surplus. A number of assistants were engaged as instructors, among others a Frenchman who taught the young ladies drawing, painting and French. One of the pupils, Miss Mary

Ann Stephenson, painted a vase of flowers on velvet, which has retained its colors to this day. Other instructors gave lessons in sewing, embroidery and last but not least deportment. A wooden wing was eventually built in order to house some of the boarders more comfortably, but unfortunately a fire probably starting in this same wing destroyed their Utopia and the "Gover Seminary," became a thing of the past.

Fisheries on the Susquehanna.—In that part of Harford County between Havre de Grace and Darlington, may be seen a number of large substantial stone houses and the observer may wonder as he looks at them, how mere farmers could afford to build such expensive luxurious dwellings. The answer is that they were built years ago on the proceeds of an immense fishing industry at Lapidum and not by farmers in any sense of the word.

From earliest times as far as we know, the bay and the river teemed with fish and the Indians were no doubt adepts in catching them. In their early land sales to the Whites, the shores along the lower river were not sold, but were to be retained forever by the Indians as fishing grounds. The poor deluded creatures!

The late Mr. Albert P. Silver states that in 1760, Henry Stump was owner of fishing rights along the shore below Lapidum, where the ice houses used to stand. This was exceedingly profitable to him and was the first attempt at fishing here on a large scale. Stump's dwelling was back from the river and behind these old ice houses. Fish were carried at the time on horses' backs in straw panniers and often a row of a hundred horses could be seen tied to the bushes waiting their turn in being loaded with fish. On an occasion such as this, one of the straw panniers was set on fire for a joke. In 1800 at Lapidum, the fish were caught in

such incredible numbers, that the surplus was used as
fertilizer and such was the smell, that a law was passed
in 1810 requiring proprietors to remove offal from the
shores. There were four fishing places on Roberts
Island and three on Spensers Island and two on Woods
Island and two on Snake Island. This island was
fished by Benjamine Silver with forty men and in one
season he produced a pack of 1600 barrels of herring.
The enormous value of these islands for fishing, is disclosed by a remark made by John W. Spencer in certain
testimony. He said he would not take as many silver
dollars for the island as would cover it, unless they
were placed on edge.

The fishing industry reached its peak between 1820
and 1830, when a man named Asahel Bailey from Havre
de Grace, invented the "Float." Before this all the
fishing had been done from the shore, but now the
float revolutionized the industry and gave scope to the
use of much longer seines. Bailey sold his float in 1830
to Benjamine and David Silver and they and their
descendants for many years were intimately connected
with this work at Lapidum. The floats gradually
increased and crowded out the shore seines and batteries
and the number of fish caught in them was simply
incredible. One float owner reported a six hundred
barrel haul at Watson's Island and even so, many
escaped; he also said that when he pulled in the seine
the fish seemed as thick on one side as the other. Several
four hundred barrel hauls were also recorded here.
Shad decreased quite rapidly in proportion to the herring. In the early fishing days shad were caught in
batteries as far up the river as Columbia and at a handsome profit to the owners.

Fish Wagons.—While these enormous hauls of fish
were being brought ashore, the news spread like wild-

fire and persons from all over this county and even from York and Lancaster Counties flocked to the scene and eager to buy them. These York and Lancaster County farmers arrived every Spring when the herring were "Running," each in his canvas topped wagon, the family, whiskey and dog inside, prepared to buy plenty of herring and to have a glorious time. They also brought with them a keg of salt for preserving the fish. On arriving at Lapidum they would buy fish, load them on their wagons and return to Pennsylvania, leaving a trail of heads and offal all the way, as the fish were opened and cleaned on their journey back home. Between 1820 and 1830 when the fishing industry was at its height, the innkeepers on the lower river did a thriving business in housing and feeding all these people, as they usually stayed two or three days before returning. The fish although growing always less plentiful year by year, attracted the Pennsylvanians even as late as 1870 and 1880. An old Darlington resident told me, that he counted at one time one hundred and ten wagons blocking the road leading to Lapidum. These white topped wagons were not Conestoga wagons, but were similarly rigged with canvas tops over wooden bows and at the rear end the canvas was puckered in with a string. The wagons were often pulled by four horses, as I have seen them myself in 1900 passing through Darlington in groups of two or three, something like gypsy caravans. The descendants of these same farmers still come to Rock Run and Lapidum each year for fish which they buy for about two cents each, but they do not come now in covered wagons.

The Monastery at Priest's Ford.—Situated on the south bank of the Deer Creek and three miles North of Churchville, stands what is known today as the Trap-

pist Monastery. It is now occupied by the Misses
Harlan who not only told me what they themselves knew
of the former papist owners, but also allowed me access
to a paper written by Dr. George W. Archer and read
before the Harford County Historical Society in 1889
on this subject. They have my thanks.

In order to understand why a Papist Chapel was
built on the hill here, it must be known that the
Catholics have always been in the minority in Maryland. In spite of this, the Assembly at St. Mary's in
1649, published what they called "The Toleration Act,"
granting freedom of worship to all. However, when the
Catholic James II was deposed and the Protestant
William and Mary ascended the throne, the Toleration
Act was repealed (1692) and the Church of England became firmly established in Maryland. All persons were
required to pay part of their taxes for the maintenance
of this church. Stringent laws were also passed against
dissenters, the Papists in particular and in 1704 a
particularly odious law went through the Assembly
forbidding Catholic priests from exercising their pro-
fessions or teaching youth in public places; and if any
of them were caught doing so would be returned to
England for trial. This law however was soon softened
down and priests were allowed to preach and teach in
a quiet way in private houses. The Assembly about
this time passed another law, prohibiting any corpora-
tion or society religious or otherwise, from holding land
without a license; but the priests avoided this issue, by
buying land from the Indians and at a distance. This
scheme worked well for a short time, but to be brief.

Between 1740 and 1747 a Jesuit Father named
Bennett Neale settled on the Deer Creek at the monastery. Whether or not he built the monastery no one
knows; at all events "The Mission of St. Joseph" ap-

pears here at this time and was known locally as "Priest
Neale's Mass House." The building stands on the hilltop overlooking the Deer Creek. It is massively built
of stone with walls a yard thick. The ceiling beams
now hidden by plaster, are of walnut and exceedingly
heavy. The building measures twenty-six by forty-six
feet and is one and a half stories high. Rumor has it
that one of the priests lies buried under the front door
and even today no colored person will sleep in the house
for fear of his ghost. Father Neale owned four or five
slaves whom he used on his one hundred and sixty
acres and from legal records, he seems to have lived on
the premises from 1747 to 1756. How much longer is
not known. He died in 1781 in St. Mary's County.
There were other priests who are mentioned in the
legal records, such as Ignatius Mathews and Father
Dedrick. The latter was attended by a doctor from
time to time and was possibly recuperating from over-
work in some other part. In 1747 the Nottingham
Forge was in operation probably at the site of Hus-
bands Mill and the "Hands" being largely Irish it is
quite possible that Father Neale or a predecessor,
settled here in order to administer to the spiritual needs
of this group of men, as they no doubt needed it. The
Lancaster Forge also was close to the monastery at the
same time. In connection with the mission there was a
grist mill, its ruins being located about one hundred
and fifty yards below the present pike and on the South
side of the road. The race may easily be seen today
and two, three-foot millstones lie partly buried in the
earth near it. The mission-farm paid the resident
priest twenty-four pounds Sterling a year toward his
support. In 1811, it was decided by the authorities at
Georgetown College to sell the estate, which was done
in 1814 being bought at that time by Dr. James Glas-

gow whose descendants have owned it ever since. The
doctor never operated the mill and the name of "Glasgow Mill" has thus no special significance. One quarter
of a mile West of the Monastery is the graveyard. There
are many graves marked with field stones but only one of
marble on which was any inscription. This one happens
to be broken and when pieced together, reads, "I. H. S.
In Memory of James Cain who was born on the 9th day
of March in ye year of God 1752 and he departed life on
ye 15th of April 1797. Age 45. May he rest in Peace."
The stone itself has now disappeared. The graveyard
lies near the edge of the woods and the stones may be
seen easily from the house. It is said that Margaret
Stump who lived where the Janneys formerly lived, often
attended chapel at St. Josephs. When the old chapel
was sold in 1814, the present chapel at Hickory was built
although the exact date is unknown. The Monastery
is located at "Priests Ford" as is generally believed,
but this is an error. The real Priests' Ford is some
distance down the creek near the bend and near the
edge of the Harlan property. Three large tulip trees
stand guard there today. The Trappist Church as far
as records show, has always been a Protestant Church;
the first building being erected in 1761 and the first
order of Trappist did not arrive in the United States
until 1803. The real priests ford while not used in
connection with the so-called Trappist Church which
would have been illegal even if there had been any
Trappists here, was used by the priests in traveling to
and from the various iron works up and down the
Creek, unobtrusively giving spiritual consolation to the
men in their homes. There were seven of these forges
on the lower creek and they must have kept the priests
busy.

Trappe Church.—I have generously helped myself to information published in the Bel Air Times, for June 1934 and written by J. Marley Cass. He has my thanks.

On the repeal of the already mentioned "Toleration Act," in 1692, the State was divided into Parishes under the jurisdiction of the Church of England. Baltimore County, including Harford and several of the others, was divided into three Parishes, the Eastern one being called St. George's Parish. The first building on the site at Trappe was erected in 1761 and called the Church of St. James. It was constructed at least partly of brick and stood here for twenty years before the English yoke was thrown off. At this time the Parish took on the name of "Deer Creek Parish," unfortunately the early records are not to be found. A scant two miles to the south was situated the Jesuit Chapel built just a few years before St. James, but having no connection with it, as the first order of Trappist monks did not enter the United States until 1803. The Mission of St. Joseph, massively built of stone and the little Church of St. James following the English custom, of brick. The brick were probably burnt near the site, as there is a great deal of very red clay quite near. Perhaps this determined the location, or perhaps it was built in order to offset the influence of the other; we will hope the former.

Lafayette and his troops marched past St. James footsore and weary in 1781 on their way to the South and also past the Mission of St. Joseph two miles further along; each in a different way an exponent of the teaching, Peace on Earth Good Will towards Men, but neither knowing quite what to do about it. Captain Graeme, who returned from the War to Harford County, lies buried in the little overgrown Churchyard. During the Revolution and in the few years following,

the country was naturally in a turmoil and the Church
falling into disrepair, the bricks were hauled off by the
wagon load and built into some of the chimneys in the
neighborhood. This was the condition of the Church
in 1800 and as it was not immediately rebuilt and the
community feeling the need of spiritual guidance after
the war, some of the parishioners attended service at·
Rock Spring (1805), some at Havre de Grace (1809),
and some at the old Church of St. George, (Spesutia)
at Perryman.

A frame building was finally erected at Trappe and
Mary Worthington was the first to be baptized in it.
Rev. Edward A. Colburn was made rector and a new
Rectory was built at a cost of eighteen hundred dollars.
Church activities now for some reason began shifting
to Darlington and some services were held in the old
Academy, when a fire occurred at Trappe in 1869 completely destroying the second building. Dr. W. B.
Everett the new Rector, held service in the adjoining
school building until under the initiative of J. C. Neilson
and a few others, a third church was built on the spot
in 1875, but owing to a shortage of funds due no doubt
to the post war depression the rectory had to be sold to
pay expenses. Today the building is completely
stripped. The Grace Memorial Church at Darlington,
built by D. C. Wharton Smith in 1876 in memory of
his father Milton Smith, is undoubtedly substantial
enough to last many years and should be a continual
inspiration to its parishioners.

Rock Run Church.—The following information, has
been gleaned from the writings of Miss Jennette C.
Parker, whose ancestors founded the Methodist Church
at Rock Run.

In the old Inn at Perryville, close to the river side,
lived at one time a man by the name of William Ste-

phenson. He was proprietor of the Inn and entertained among other guests, George Washington and
Lafayette when they passed down the Old Post Road
before his door. In 1780, growing tired of hotel life, he
removed to Harford County and bought a tract of land
above Rock Run from John Stump. There was a one
room log cabin on the property, which Mr. Stephenson
immediately began enlarging, but unfortunately died
before he could enjoy it. His family consisted of his
widow and six children. William, one of the sons,
inherited the homestead and married in due time,
Hetty Parker.

In the year 1783 John and Charles Wesley were tour-
ing the Eastern Seaboard in the interest of Methodism
and some of their satellites were doing missionary work
in the wilder sections of the country. One of these
revivals was held at Calvary, which was attended
among hundreds of others, by young William Stephenson and his family. They were much encouraged by
the number of converts obtained here and arranged the
next meeting to be held at William Stephenson's home
on the River hill and such was the attendance that it is
said the line of horses and vehicles extended clear to
Level. Believe this or not, it was at this meeting that
William Stephenson became converted to Methodism.
He now formed the habit of evening Bible reading with
the family, which soon included a number of neighbors.
These meetings were held under trees as the house was
not large enough to accommodate that number of
people. Two candles were placed near his Bible and a
small colored boy was entrusted with snuffers to keep
the wicks the proper length. Stephenson was finally
ordained a minister and he officiated at marriages held
at his house and at burials of some of the neighbors,
and he allowed them the use of his family graveyard

nearby. This was then much more extensive than it is today, for at that time the gravestones stood well beyond the road. Rev. Stephenson owned slaves, but not believing it altogether right to keep them, set them free. By 1810 these religious gatherings grew so large that it was decided to build a church which was to be used in part as a school. The site chosen stood on the line between the land of Mr. Stephenson and Smith his neighbor and close to a spring of water. It lay also near the road from Level to Stafford and close to the present dwelling of the Misses Parker. A school was equally necessary, for though the "Gover Seminary" stood not far away, it only gave instruction to young ladies. The building was of stone and was built by the Bowman and Baily families. A schoolmaster from New England was engaged named Samuel Guild, who gave faithful service here until his death in 1821. His body lies in the burying ground on the hill. Little is known of the early activities of either the church or school, but it is said that Mr. Guild held school from "Sun up until sun down" and only gave two weeks' holiday in the year. On his death, the school was abandoned and the instruction continued by William Stephenson's five daughters at their home. On William's demise, the daughters built near their dwelling a board schoolhouse, the establishment assuming the name of "Belmont Seminary." Elizabeth the eldest of the five, was the moving spirit; mathematics was taught, also geography, history and mythology. A two months' vacation was given to the pupils and this in Winter because of the severity of the weather. The stone building near the road however continued to serve as a church until 1843, when owing to the increase in membership the present Rock Run Church was built and by Joshua W. Stevens on land donated by

James Stephenson, a nephew of The Rev. William Stephenson. The original stone church on the Elbow Branch road is now but a heap of stones and the pedestrian who occasionally passes, little knows the important part it has played in early Harford County Methodism.

Ferries over the Susquehanna River.—My thoughts often turn to the quaint story of old Anteus and the Pigmies and the fearful battle he fought against Hercules. In this battle which I will briefly recount, Anteus was thrown to the earth time after time by Hercules, to the infinite chagrin of his staunch pigmy friends, but each time he touched the earth he arose with a strength ten times that which he possessed before, until finally Hercules dispairing of conquering such an opponent, caught him around the waist and held him above the earth until his strength slowly ebbed away. Many of us today are in the same predicament. We are prevented from renewing our contact with old Mother Earth by a giant far stronger than Hercules, to wit, the pressure of the Twentieth Century. We are a race of mechanical geniuses and to use momentarily the well known phrases have built for ourselves a Frankenstein, which is depriving us of our birthright and preventing us from gaining the strength which we so sadly need.

From earliest times, streams and rivers have presented almost insurmountable barriers to travel. The Nanticokes of Early Maryland were proficient in building bridges and there are several names such as "Indian Bridge," "Indian Bridge Point," "Indian Bridge Neck" on modern maps today. There were approximately twenty-three Indian bridges in Eastern Maryland and also some in Virginia (William B. Marye). Before passing, I wish to mention that streams and rivers also presented more or less impassable barriers to forest fires and we can thank the streams and our colonial beaver for their share in preserving the forests.

A bridge is often a frail and usually an expensive means of crossing water. How much simpler a boat, each man paying for what he gets in transportation service. At Havre de Grace in 1715, there was some kind of a ferry, as we discover from laws passed in that year requiring all persons leaving the Province to give three months' notice by affixing same to the Courthouse door. This was to catch tax dodgers. And furthermore as certain "ill-minded persons" residing at the head of the Bay have "set people over" for some small profit, from now on, a license will be required for the transportation of any passenger. This was in order to hinder runaway slaves. This ferry was known later as the "Susquehanna Lower Ferry."

At Lapidum, a few miles up the river and at the site of the old ice houses, was situated in 1720 what was known as "Harrises Landing." There was no ferry here then and the landing was for the convenience of numerous tobacco shippers who rolled tobacco to the dock. Edward Harris owned this property, as he had fallen heir to it from Daniel Johnson and some time later it passed in turn to Nathan Rigbie and for the same purpose.

About the year 1727, Thomas Cresap celebrated his nuptials and settled in Cecil County on the river below Port Deposit. He soon petitioned the Court in Cecil County for the privilege of operating a ferry across the River at this point and also of building a road connecting this ferry with the Octoraro road, the journey being extremely tedious at this time without one. Both these privileges were granted. The Cecil County Rock

Run Mill had evidently been built previous to 1731, as ships came up to it to load their tobacco. The land between it and the present river bank is all "made" land. The remains of this road connecting with the Octoraro road, is still barely visible (1939) and forms the northern limit to the property now owned by Peter Tome, and ascends the hill in the ravine between it and the large granite quarry.

These early ferry boats were very crude, being often dug-out canoes and often in transporting a wagon two of them were fastened together. In 1730 Cresap moved up the river to the "Blue Rock Ferry" and Miles Foy probably continued its operation for a certain time. He died in 1751, his house being situated on the side of the hill above it. The ferry at Harris Landing was abandoned about 1737 and was operated by William Perkins after this date, but further up the river. It was known now as "Perkins Ferry" and Perkins continued to operate it until his death in 1760. Reuben Perkins, his son, now fell heir to the enterprise, living in a stone house located a short distance above Dr. Verdin's dwelling. The road to this ferry descended the hill by the present lane and leaving it a short distance below the dwelling, followed the ravine past the old spring house to the river bank. The name "Perkins Ferry," gradually gave way to "Smith's Ferry," as Thomas Smith succeeded Perkins in 1772 and probably lived in the same house. Smith kept an Inn at Lapidum for the use of travelers and during the Revolutionary War assisted in transporting troops when they were on their way from the Head of Elk River to Baltimore and Yorktown. There is one record at this time of rent for one of his flat boats for eight days, at three shillings nine pence a day and another to Mr. Creswell of Cecil County, for the use of his flats for

NOBLE'S GRIST MILL

eight days, at five shillings a day. John Creswell lived
at Port Deposit and operated "Creswell's Ferry" which
may have had its terminus at Havre de Grace. Thomas
Smith built part of the late Dr. Verdin's residence and
lived there until 1791, when he died. The next ferry
owner was Robert Bell; the ferry name now becoming
"Bells Ferry" as might be imagined. He moved here
in 1793 two years after Smith's demise, and continued
to run the boats and the Inn until about 1807, when his
son Robert, took over the business. Robert being
enterprising, moved the Harford End up to the mouth
of Herring Run and the old house at the end of the
bridge was his ferry house. He also installed a horsepower boat which was also equipped with sails; this
boat was really two boats fastened side by side, one for
the power and one for the passengers and freight.
In 1818 there were two such boats in use here but
owing to the erection at that time of the "Rock Run
Port Deposit Bridge" the ferry trade gradually diminished. The name of "Bells Ferry" was now abandoned
and the name of "Lapidum" took its place, the spot
being christened by Dr. Robert H. Archer.

Beginning in 1840 with the "Canton," a fleet of
steamboats one after another now make their appearance, plying between Lapidum and Port Deposit and
then Havre de Grace. After the "Canton" came the
"Gosport" and in 1848 the "Cecil." In 1850 the "Port
Deposit" was put in service, then in 1854 the "Gypsy"
in opposition to the latter. After these a boat called
"The Ferry" assumed its duties (1860) and two years
later, the "Rodman." Next in order comes the
"Isadore" and then "Alice," which was operated from
1864 until 1868. For the next few years there was no
steamboat on this route, but 1872 the "Maggie" was
put in service under Captain Bailey; then came the

"McCall" and in 1878 the "Benigna" and she, after ten years service to Port Deposit, gave way for the last, the "City Belle," who after as many years more service, met her fate by fire at Havre de Grace about 1905.

This information, I have shamelessly borrowed from the paper of Mr. Albert P. Silver on "Lapidum," and I am sure he would not have objected in having these few facts passed on.

Susquehanna and Tidewater Canal.—The following information is taken from a paper written by Daniel F. Shure and quoted in part.

The upper reaches of the "Pennsylvania Canal," having been completed in 1831, as far down as Columbia on the East side of the river; an outlet on the Chesapeake was naturally the next step, in order to obtain access to the enormous timber resources of the interior. In 1824 a stock company was formed with a paid up capital of one and a half million dollars and charters were obtained from both Pennsylvania and Maryland on April 25, 1835. The survey included a dam to be built over the river at Columbia, 6700 feet long and a bridge to be used as a tow path, one mile long. The construction work was started in the Spring of 1836 and water was finally admitted three years later, in the Fall of 1839.

The construction was comprehensive in its character and proved so far beyond the estimate of its chief engineer, that the failure to meet these items in the forecast, involved the Company almost in the vortex of inextricable difficulties. But having been commenced and so far underway, had of a necessity to be surmounted at any cost however great; the sudden advance in labor and provisions and lack of suitable materials for the bed and banks of the canal, which had to be dug from the fields on the tops of the hills

(Written by Daniel F. Shure)

and dumped into expensive shutes at many points, to
the rocky bed of the canal below and then disposed of
in carts, to such points as proved to be deficient in the
proper material, were also a cause of great expense.
The failure to complete the work within the estimates
of the chief engineer, E. F. Gay, was largely due to the
frequent washing of the freshets and abrasions of the
ponderous ice floes, set in motion many times in the
Winter, doing more or less damage as often as these
occurrences took place, which had to be followed
immediately by repairs wherever practicable and in
nine cases out of ten, the superstructure was founded
on the rocky bed of the stream, which required prompt
and the most indomitable energy to keep abreast of
the work, until after the Spring of the third year; by
which time the work was reared above the danger line
of ordinary freshets. The work was finished by the
end of the fourth year, so far as to admit water late
in the Fall of 1839. (Just one hundred years ago as I
copy this.) As the character of the work and the
difficulties attending its completion, were similar
throughout, it would seem futile to reiterate what occurred in the foregoing. In order to test the relative
qualities of the bed and banks of the canal, extensive
preparations were made for the grand opening. Re-
lays of horses and drivers were stationed along the line
upon this great occasion. Among those present, were
some of the most distinguished persons in Pennsylvania
and Maryland. It was on that occasion, that the
Honorable Nicholas Biddle of Philadelphia, made his
famous speech on internal improvements from the
wing wall of the outlet lock at Havre de Grace, then a
subject of paramount importance. The excursion was
a great success, but the gentlemen composing it, had
hardly reached their respective homes, when disas-

(Written by Daniel F. Shure)

trous breaks occurred, extending along the greater part
of the line and the most extensive one, which occurred
at the Otter Creek aqueduct at York Furnace. The
cause of this was owing to the defects in the preparation and puddling of the same. The bed and banks of
the canal, are held in place by wing abutments and
retaining walls of huge blocks of granite, thirty-five
feet above the bed of the river. The interval embracing
this work, is four miles long, fifty feet wide and six feet
deep, and where a body of water occupying so large an
area gains egress through an artificial earth structure,
it instantly becomes irresistible, leaving nothing behind
but absolute destruction, even the heavy blocks of
stone were carried some distance into the river. Although this break was much the largest of the series,
it nevertheless cost less to repair it than the aggregate
cost of the numerous small breaks. It was very unfortunate that these disasters should have occurred at
a time when there was no money in the treasury, no
credit and the Company deeply involved in debt.
Means were nevertheless availed by the directors upon
their individual responsibility and the repairs were
made during the Winter and the canal was formally
opened to the public in the Spring of 1840, at an approximate cost of four million dollars. Four of the units of
work were as follows:

(1) Towpath bridge at Columbia.......... $ 90,000
(2) Columbia dam...................... 220,000
(3) Conestoga dam (now abandoned)...... 100,000
(4) From Lapidum to Havre de Grace..... 500,000

These units alone, totaled $910,000 of the million and a
half dollars subscribed.

Numerous points of bold rocky bluffs were blasted
away, in order to reduce the radius within the lines of

(Written by Daniel F. Shure)

free and easy navigation. Deep pools and chasms were filled and crossed over upon superstructures of huge oak timbers, adjusted longitudinally several feet below the lowest stage of the river, on which many of the high vertical walls are found today and remain intact, except below Conowingo, a hundred feet of which slipped from its footing into "Job's Hole," fifty feet deep in 1861 and although the wall has not been rebuilt, the notch permanently closed and is quite as reliable as before the occurrence took place.

During the season of 1840, trade on the Canal was limited and the revenue was proportionately small; owing in a great degree to the want of integrity of the embankments, throwing the Canal idle much of the time. There was also a want of boats to move the coal and lumber, which had already accumulated for shipment to tidewater. The trade, soon however began to increase rapidly and for many years, until it reached its maximum in 1870, when it was largely divided by competition and gradually diminished by reason of new railroad lines entering the region and tapping the sources of trade developed by the opening of the "Susquehanna and Tidewater Canal." During the interval between 1840 and 1870, the capacity of the Canal was increased in its depth, from three feet to six feet and the cargoes from 70 tons to 150 tons, which is the present capacity. The Canal occupies an interval from Columbia to Havre de Grace, of forty-five miles of the Susquehanna. There are twenty-nine locks, eighteen farm and road bridges, nine aqueducts, twenty-eight waste weirs and four dams, two across the river and one across each of the creeks, Muddy and Deer Creek. The locks are 170 feet long and sixteen and a half feet wide. In June 1872 the Reading Railroad leased the Canal and have operated it ever since.

(Written by Daniel F. Shure. Previous to its abandonment in 1890.)

The Canal Boat Hands and the Lock Keepers of the
Susquehanna and Tidewater Canal dwelt in a world
apart, the fishermen and river "rats" being their
satellites. Life here was happy and thoroughly satis-
factory. Barges passed and repassed going up and
down, now in the shadow of overhanging trees and next
in the glare of the hot sun and always the company of
the grand old river with its countless rapids and sunny
islands.

Between Havre de Grace and the Pennsylvania line
at Peach Bottom, there were eleven locks, each with
its separate lock keeper who lived close by in a whitewashed house each one typical of the river. At Peach
Bottom beginning at the State Line, the lock in 1889 was
tended by a man named Thomas Richie. A mile
above "Broad Creek," lived William Fulton; below
"Broad Creek," John J. Barrow. Immediately below
the end of the Conowingo Bridge was Theodore Richie;
one mile below Glen Cove lived George Brown. One
half mile below Hopkins Branch lived Joseph Bostic
and it went by the name of the Bostic's Lock. At
Shures Landing dwelt William Spense who tended lock
here. At the head of Deer Creek Island lived Phillip
McGibboney, successor to John W. Hawkins. At the
foot of Deer Creek Island lived William Clark; at
Lapidum was Roy Price, whose lock was called Ste-
phensons Lock and finally Mitchel's Lock at Havre de
Grace, the name of the tender being unknown to me.

On the approach of a canal boat, a conch shell was
blown by the captain and the lock keeper closed the
necessary gates, crossing the lock on a plank pivoted
near one end and weighted with stones so as to swing
across easily. When the boat or boats were in the lock
the gates were swung shut, the lower ports opened
and water admitted or let out as the case might be,

until the boats had reached the new level when the gates themselves were opened and the boats were at liberty to continue on their way.

The Canal Company owned a number of these boats and in addition there were boats owned by private parties who used the canal at a yearly rental. One of these had painted on its stern, first a large letter "R," then a painting of a "Can," next the butt end of a "Saw," and finally a little man carrying a valise. This masterpiece being interpreted, indicating the "Arkansaw Traveler." The name of the owner is unfortunately lost. The "Indian Hunter," was owned by a man named John Steel. This particular boat rotted away at the Paper Mill dock. Richard Councilman owned a double boat (two boats). Jerry Crowley owned one. Cooney Serrick from Pennsylvania owned one and Jake Umschweiler and a man named Crownshied both from Pennsylvania each owned double boats and finally Captain Charlie White, who ran a scow for the Paper Mill and hauled lumber and coal and other supplies and lived near by at Castleton. The Company's boats were unnamed.

Mules were used for hauling these Canal boats. One pair was the usual number for a single boat and four head for double boats and sometimes six head were used, but never one mule. When two boats met, the one ascending the canal kept to the tow path, the cable being unhooked from the double tree of the descending team and as the cable sank in the water, the up boat glided over it. There was an enormous tonnage hauled on the canal as may easily be appreciated from the size of the warehouses along the banks.

The article by Daniel F. Shure, was written before the occurrence of the more violent floods. At the time of the Johnstown flood in 1889 large sections of the

canal bank washed out. One of the largest, was below
the end of the Conowingo bridge which he mentions as
washing out in 1861 and never being properly replaced
with stone. Canal boats were stranded in the mud
after this flood, from one end to the other and in order
to get their expensive cargoes to their destinations
hundreds of men were employed in repairing the
breaks. One hundred men were put on this Conowingo
break alone. The Company soon began to realize that
the maintenance of the Canal was a very expensive
affair and became quite certain of it in 1890, when the
canal banks were so badly damaged in a flood occurring
in that year, that as a whole it was definitely abandoned. The lower part however, continued for a few
years more, when it was also abandoned.

Lumber industry of the lower Susquehanna.—Our
grandfathers were right when they spoke of the immense resources of the United States; its inexhaustible
forests, its streams teeming with fish, its coal, its iron,
and its abundant game and what more natural reaction
than to exploit these resources, before it was done by
someone else. Thus began a regime of despoilation
by rifle, axe and fire, that has probably not been
equaled on the face of the Earth. Our ancestors were
told by Francis Scott Key, that they lived in the land
of the free and he told them so only too truly. He told
them also that they were brave and some of them undoubtedly were but he failed to mention however, that
they were damn fools, for they were. Who but a damn
fool or lunatic would cut his own throat and watch his
life blood ebbing away. Today we haven't the natural
resources to despoil. The stable doors are open and
the horse has gone.

In order to appreciate the tragedy caused by the

wasteful cutting of our Pennsylvania White Pine, it is necessary for us to see these trees growing in their primeval habitat. "Virgin Stands" are today exceedingly rare. There is one tract of 4000 acres containing hemlock and pine on Tionesta Creek, in North Western Pennsylvania, which has been fortunately preserved by the government. This achievement was consummated by the Herculean efforts of Mr. Francis R. Cope of Montrose, Pennsylvania, who had vision enough and energy enough to save this last "Stand," before the "Central Pennsylvania Lumber Company" had laid it low in the usual style, as they are doing as rapidly as possible on adjoining tracts.

In the early years of the last century, the white pine from New York was cut and floated down the Mohawk to Albany. Those forests contiguous to the headwaters of the Delaware, were rafted down that stream; but it was not until 1807 that the enormous white pine forests along the Susquehanna were cut in a really big way. In that year two brothers named Phelps took the first log rafts down the Susquehanna to tidewater from Owego, New York. The exhilaration and delight of such a journey may easily be imagined.

In the year 1822, five hundred and nineteen lumber Arks came down the Susquehanna and in addition three hundred and sixty-three made the trip past the rapids, via the Susquehanna Canal. These Arks and rafts were brought ashore at Port Deposit, where there was every imaginable kind of saw mill and planing mill to handle this huge business. During the months of March and April of 1823, there was a tidy business done at Port Deposit to the amount of $1,337,925.00. In those two months, one hundred and twenty-six vessels entered and cleared at their docks. Most of the business was lumber; but wheat, whiskey and iron,

were also handled. Besides the lumber and other local
products, about two million shingles were brought down
by boat from Michigan and Southern pine was shipped
up in schooners from Georgia which was distributed
throughout the country. Trade was also carried on
with Cuba in "Shooks" for barrels. In 1829, the
"Chesapeake and Delaware Canal" was completed,
thus giving an additional impetus to trade, which
reached its peak at Port Deposit, between 1833 and
1840.

White Pine was the most valuable timber cut at this
time, but Spruce and Hemlock were also cut though of
less value. In 1850, lumbering started on the West
branch at Lock Haven and two years later at Williamsport. It has been estimated that between the years
1851 and 1876, some six million lineal feet of logs were
cut, which denuded an area roughly of twenty-one
hundred square miles. The inevitable fires which
followed, not only crippled or destroyed the uncut
trees but burnt what is almost of more value, the
thirty inch layer of rich black humus which is necessary
as a seed bed for more young pines. When this is
burnt off, the roots of the pine stumps stand exposed
as if on stilts and the soil is now only suitable for de-
ciduous trees such as field birch and maple and scrub
oak. At these saw mills at Williamsport, a cut of
twenty million feet of boards was produced annually
and most of it floated down the river in Arks to be sold
at Port Deposit.

Rafts made of logs cut at other places such as on the
Loyalsock Creek at Muncey came down also, with
dogs barking and the Monday wash flying. These log
rafts were built twelve logs wide with cross poles
stapled on to hold them in place; often two or three
rafts were chained together end to end. In the bow

two long sweeps were set and two more at the stern for guiding the affair through the rapids. The Pilots of the rafts took their families often with them where they lived in a shack on one of the sections and as was before stated, the family wash often hung out to dry in the sun and wind. When the rafts reached their destination at Port Deposit the logs were sold and the pilots went up to their village on Bell's Hill which is known as Pilot today.

The Susquehanna River, unlike the Delaware, has its shoals and rapids near the mouth and many rafts went afoul on the last stretch. Out of a total of two thousand or twenty-five hundred rafts sent down each year, possibly only one thousand and sometimes only five hundred arrived at their destination. These losses occurred after the Susquehanna Canal was abandoned in 1836. At Lock Haven there were impounding "Booms," capable of holding two hundred million board feet. These "Booms" were formed of floating logs, chained end to end and stretching across the river. Freshets played havoc with them, often bursting the chain couplings and thus liberating the whole contents, which would go careening off on its journey to the bay, where little of it was ever recovered. There were always stray logs in the river and saw mills sprang up along its shores which sawed them into boards. Men known as "Algerines," collected the logs and sold them to the mills and thus formed the basis of many a family fortune. Besides the lumber business conducted at Port Deposit, must be added its granite industry and its fisheries, which later was of no mean dimension. In 1832, the Susquehanna Canal Company enlarged its log pond above Port Deposit and near the present baseball field, to handle the increase in business. There were saw mills located both at Conowingo and at

Octoraro and some grist mills below these sites all drawing water from the canal. The company objected to the amount of water used by these mills. It also objected to wheeled vehicles using the tow path and had barriers placed at intervals to prevent this kind of traffic. As these sketches are supposed to be concerned only with Harford County I will not prolong this article but turn to other matters.

Some of the above information was gleaned from an article written by Richard R. Griffith and published in the "Baltimore Sun" in 1934.

Cookville.—A mile and a half West of Glenville on Mill Brook, is situated one of the quaintest little settlements that could be found in a day's journey. Here with his sister, lives George P. Cook, a member of the Society of Friends and now well over eighty years of age. The property was bought by his grandfather, Elisha, in 1816 and the weatherboard log dwelling is said to have looked as old then as it does today. Elisha Cook was a man of energy and after organizing his farm, immediately began building a dam and race, which was to furnish power for a spinning and weaving mill, built under the hill and near the dwelling. The ruins of the mill are visible today and measure twenty by forty feet. Here was spun and woven woolen cloth produced from fleeces brought by farmers from the adjoining farms. The mill continued in operation until about 1850, when not being able to compete with modern spinning mills was forced to shut down. In 1842 Elisha built a small stone house near the public road, where he settled his son, George P. Cook, as a storekeeper and who kept store on the ground floor for forty years. During this time, not being thoroughly content to wait for trade, George built a tanbark mill across the brook near the road and a dwelling for the operator opposite to it. Black Oak bark was procured, hauled to the bark mill and broken into small pieces by hand. It was then thrown into an iron hopper and a horse which was led onto the second floor from the hillside, walked round and around grinding the bark to a powder, which fell through into a cart below. The present owner when a boy, often assisted in breaking the bark in pieces and feeding the hopper and was instructed by his uncle George, to throw in every piece that had two ends. Cow hides were bought locally and at one time a salted shipment came from South America. These hides were first laced together and then run through a vat containing limewater in order to remove the hair. They were then put down in the tan pits which are visible today, and tan liquor poured over them and allowed to lie for nearly a year. Several times during this period the men "Turned Pack," that is, they removed the hides and put them back another way, thus allowing all parts to be evenly tanned. When the process was completed the hides were hung along the fences on both sides of the road to drain and dry and were in this condition sold to manufacturers of shoes and leather belting.

The stone house as mentioned before, was used as a store on the ground floor. The second floor was used as a private school, the teacher being George P. Cook's sister. School was taught by her until 1862, when the store below was given up and the whole building devoted to the use of a public school and run as such for a number of years. The present owner George P. Cook, and William Silver among others were pupils here.

Today the weaving mill ruins are barely visible; the bark mill, the operator's house and the schoolhouse, are mellow with age, but the owner, George P. Cook, although over eighty years old is still able to hold his own with the boys (1939).

Brüningers Tan Yard.—We now come to a few reminiscences told me in 1933 by our friend and neighbor Fred C. Jones. About the year 1890 there lived at the head of the Castleton quarry a German, by the name of Brüninger. Now Mr. Brüninger could speak very little English, although he had a fine bass voice which he used to exercise on Sunday at the Franklin Church nearby. He also wore earrings and smoked in his leisure a meerschaum pipe. Whether it was his voice or the earrings or the pipe, the fact remains that he boasted of having had four wives and at the time of this narrative, the fourth wife was all that remained. Below his house, which stood quite high on the lower side were some fine slate flags and the last Mrs. Brüninger decided that no better place could be found for committing suicide than right on those flags. She thereupon opened an upper window and leaped out, but just as she fell, her doughty husband seeing the flash of skirts, left his chair below and springing forward seized her by the ankle, but to his chagrin all to no avail, for as he explained later, "My suspenders broke and I had to let her go."

Brüninger operated a tan yard here for some years, having first served an apprenticeship at Moore's Tan Yard, which stood near the dwelling of Mr. Heighe on Bynum Run below Bel Air. He next worked for George P. Cook at Cookville in the same capacity. Just below the tan yard is the flint quarry owned at that time probably by the Smiths. However, a man named Burkins was in charge and every time a dynamite blast went off, a shower of stones and rubbish descended on Brüninger's roof. He made frequent complaints to Mr. Burkins, but as he said whenever he protested, Mr. Burkins would say "Hell" and walk away.

The Reynolds Tract.—Somewhere in the Greenstone outcrop above Dublin, is a very deep mine, where iron ore was quarried in old days. After the completion of the Columbia and Port Deposit Railroad, it occurred to some one to open up the old mine and get out iron in order to make a little pin money. This ore he proposed shipping from Conowingo on the railroad. He thereupon began hauling the material down past Castleton and down the old road which used to descend the river hills at the end of Conowingo Bridge. He had an old wagon and hauled light loads. On one of these trips just as he started on the grade to the River, his wagon broke down and his interest in iron probably at the same time. At all events, in order to repair the wagon, he threw off the ore in a hole at one side of the road, where it lay for some years.

In Cecil County, there lived at the time of this narrative, an energetic man by the name of Reynolds and understanding that many good things come from this side of the River, came across the Conowingo bridge and began hunting over the hills above, with a declination needle. Now a declination needle is a very curious thing, but like other curious things must be thoroughly understood. It is made something like a compass, but hung so that if brought over iron, the needle dips down and not to the north as with the Compass. Mr. Reynolds had as I said a declination needle. Suddenly at one side of the road just as it started on the down grade to the River, he was astonished to see his needle stand firmly on its head, thus indicating a large deposit of iron. Looking furtively around he replaced his needle and later persuaded Mr. Hugh A. Jones to sell him fifty acres at this spot, as he considered the

view far finer than anything in Cecil County. Five
hundred dollars was paid and then came the awakening.
The extensive iron deposit turned out to be the wagon
load thrown off years before, but Mr. Reynolds still
had the view. When the Power Company bought its
property on the River banks about 1920 the Reynolds'
heirs were paid back the five hundred dollars and the
account was finally balanced.

The Elephant at the Hotel.—Mr. Fred C. Jones also
told me the following anecdote. His dwelling above
Castleton was built by his father, Hugh A. Jones in
1830 as a hotel for the convenience of fishermen and also
of persons traveling North or South over the Conowingo
Bridge. One evening, what was their astonishment to
see walking up the road by the house, an elephant,
driven by a man with a small dog. He stopped at the
hotel and asked board and lodging for himself, dog and
elephant. Mr. Jones being equal to any emergency,
gave the man a room and had the elephant chained
with a log chain to a sill in the shed standing near the
road. In the middle of the night a furious barking from
the dog aroused the house and on investigation, it was
found that the elephant had fallen asleep and in so
doing, had leaned against one side of the shed loosen-
ing several boards. The next morning the man mounted
his steed and padded down the hill to the bridge on his
way to Philadelphia.

Morse Sawmill.—A mile and a quarter South West of
Coopstown Church and situated on Winter's Run, is
the sawmill of the Morse family. Elijah Morse moved
into Harford County from Vermont in 1836 and being
shrewd and hard working like others from New England, forgot that he had moved South of the Mason
and Dixon Line and began a number of enterprises;
among others, a mulberry nursery, a watch repairing

OLD CONOWINGO BRIDGE

shop, where he also repaired jewelry and a sawmill.
This in 1840. The sawmill, although not unique in the
County by any means, attracted a number of interested
onlookers during the first day's cut. The saw was
known as a pit saw and Mr. Morse succeeded in sawing
over five hundred feet of boards for his first customer,
whose name was John Wood. The latter, paid one
dollar and a half a hundred feet for the sawing alone.
George Washington Morse succeeded his father and
like his famous namesake cutting cherry trees now and
then when occasion required. Mr. Morse not only cut
boards, but lath, palings and shingles as well. He also
specialized on wagon parts. In 1892 the mill caught
fire and burned down and the great question then
arose, whether to install a pit saw in the new mill or
one of the modern circular saws. The matter was
finally settled in favor of the latter and a "De Loach
Mill" was purchased in Savannah, Georgia. The opening day of the new mill and modern circular saw, again
brought the farmers to the spot, where they viewed
with amazement the humming steel slice through the
logs. Mr. Morse now added a planer, a joiner and a
lathe to his mill and finding that the stream did not
supply enough power, bought a steam engine to use
when necessary, the saw dust being burnt as fuel.
George W. Morse died in 1912 and his sons inherited
the business. A large tract of woods was now acquired
below the mill and careful cutting was done there, but
no trees under twelve inches in diameter were removed.
Nelson Morse is the lumberman today and still con-
tinues work at the old spot, where he has the enviable
distinction of operating probably the oldest sawmill in
the United States.

At this point it may be well to give a short account of
power saws and their development, for from this in-

formation it may be possible to approximately date houses containing sawed timbers. One of the earliest power sawmills was situated in Augsburg, Germany and was operating in 1322. It was undoubtedly of the "Pit Saw" type. This type consisted of a saw approximately six feet long strained in frame of heavy oak. A crank below, caused the frame and saw to move up and down, cutting on the down stroke only. "Gang Saws," or three or more saws placed in the frame side by side, were used in Ratisbon as early as 1575. The first sawmill erected in America was at the Falls of the Piscatauqua, on the line between Maine and New Hampshire in 1634. On the Delaware, before the arrival of William Penn in 1681, the Swedes and Dutch operated these mills and in New Orleans in 1803, a steam mill was located. At this time the sharpening was considered a secret process and the sawyer did his work in a locked room. Circular saws now make their appearance. The first circular saw was patented by Samuel Miller in England on August 5, 1777, although they were said to have been in use in Holland a hundred years earlier. The first circular saw in use in America, was produced by Benjamine Cummins about 1814 at Bentonsville, New York. He made the saw at his blacksmith shop, but it was not until March 16, 1820, when Robert Eastman of Brunswick, Maine secured a patent, that circular saws came into general use in America. These early saws had square holes for the mandrel; by 1840 their development became rapid. Two years later the band saw was put on the market, having been patented by a Frenchman who after great difficulty devised a method of joining the two ends of the band so that it would not come apart when in operation. Little by little, human ingenuity has overcome these difficulties and when we picture the crude pit saw in Augsburg of 600 years ago and the marvels in steel today, we are left with varying emotions.

"The Headless Ghost" written by James W. Harry May 6, 1932 published in the Bel Air Times.

In Colonial days a familiar figure often seen in the rural districts was the peddler. These "Merchants of the Road" carried huge packs on their backs consisting of an assortment of dry-goods, notions, jewelry, and all manner of small articles for sale. They traveled on foot from hamlet to hamlet in by-ways and paths offering their goods for sale to the country folk. Besides the great pack they carried on their backs, they always had with them a stout cane or stock. This served a dual purpose of keeping vicious dogs away from them and affording a convenient means of resting their weary backs by placing the cane under the pack thus taking the weight off their backs.

The following story is about the murder of one of these peddlers whose ghost haunted the scene of his untimely death for many years afterward. I relate the story as told to me by my father whose grandfather told him the story, as related by his grandfather, an eye witness to the strange apparition.

In the upper part of Harford County, then Baltimore County, near the Susquehanna River, there is a small stream of water known today as "Peddlers Run." In the land grants of the Lord Proprietor it was called Rock Run. It was on the banks of this stream of water that the ghost of the murdered peddler appeared and kept vigilance for years, until his wants became known and his desire satisfied.

In the year 1763 John Bryarly, a small land owner and a grist mill operator was on his way one morning in the early Spring of that year. His way led along

(*Written by James W. Harry*)

the banks of the run to a mill race that carried the
water from that stream to the mill. The old mill race
can yet be plainly seen as it winds its way through the
meadow and woods to the place where the mill then
stood. He suddenly came upon the prostrate form of
a man lying in the pathway. He was horrified to
discover that the man had been murdered. The body
was headless. It was evident that the man had been
murdered by having his head severed from his body
with a sharp instrument, at a single stroke, for the cut
was clean with no ragged edges to the wound, which
would have appeared if a dull instrument had been
used. There was nothing on or about the body, that
would serve for identification. His head was nowhere
to be found. It had completely disappeared. The
hands of the murdered man indicated that he was not
of the laboring class for they were soft and free of
callous. The murder had been committed between
dark and sunrise of the previous night, for Bryarly had
passed that way the previous evening at sundown.
The identity of the murdered man remained a mystery.
He was buried where they had found his headless
trunk, by a rock, between the stream of water and the
mill race.

Some months after the finding and the burial of the
headless man, a peddler's pack was found some distance
from the scene of the murder in a clump of bushes
where it was cast. Only the canvas cover remained.
The finding of the peddler's pack and cane, associated
the murder of a few months before with a peddler. It
was thought that the murdered man must have been
one of the peddlers who frequented that section of the
country. It was recalled that at about the time of the
murder, two peddlers were seen together in the village
of Castleton, a small village a short distance down-

(Written by James W. Harry)

stream. One was carrying a large pack on his back and the other a small handbag in his hand. The one with the small handbag also carried at his waist in a scabbard, a sword. It was supposed that the murdered man had been one of the peddlers and the murderer his companion. Both were foreigners, said to have been Syrians.

Some six months after this episode, the same John Bryarly was returning home from his work in the mill by the same path in which he had found the murdered man. It was between sunset and dark when he saw a figure of a man standing at the rock where the peddler had been buried. His back was toward Bryarly and he seemed to bend forward, while he kept thrusting a cane or stick deep into the grave. He kept this up for several minutes. Bryarly was horrified to discover when the figure of the man turned toward him, that it was without a head. The headless apparition then continued along the path some three hundred yards to a swamp, where it again stopped and again thrust its cane deep into the marshy land, and after a few moments vanished from sight.

Bryarly greatly frightened at what he had seen told his neighbors about his strange experience. Others from time to time saw the same figure of a man, without a head, always at the same place and always stopping at the grave of the peddler and thrusting his cane deep into the grave and then going on to the same spot in the marsh and repeating the same operation. Great fear and consternation came upon the country folk who lived near the scene of the ghostly visitation. People avoided the place. Bryarly was forced to abandon his mill. Even the road which ran a short distance from the grave of the ghost was abandoned and a new one constructed. People passing the spot to this day walk

(Written by James W. Harry)

briskly by, automobiles gain speed as they cross the little bridge that now spans the stream. The name of the run was changed from "Rock Run" to that of "Peddler's Run." At night the place is strangely quiet except for the hooting of the owl, the barking of the fox, the gurgling of the brook. The ghost of the peddler need no longer be feared. It has vanished from the locality. It is at peace and at rest. The disappearance of the ghost of Peddler's Run was brought about in the following manner.

In the Spring of 1843, Joseph Warner, the owner of the farm on which the grave of the headless ghost was dug, was engaged in digging a ditch from the run to the head of a swamp for the purpose of draining the marshy land. While digging near where the ghost was always seen poking his cane into the ground, four feet down from the surface, he came across the skull of a man. It had been severed from the body, the cut was clean, with no ragged edges to the bone. It had been buried with the top of the skull downward. The story of the murdered man was recalled and the finding of the headless body. It was thought that the murderer had picked up the head of his victim and had cast it into a spring of water the night the murder had been committed. Warner had the grave of the peddler opened, placed the skull on the skeleton, and in a new oak box reburied the bones of the peddler in the original grave beside the rock. Since then the "Headless Ghost of Peddler's Run" has not been seen. It was quite evident that the soul of the murdered one could not rest while his body was in one place and his head in another, and in the very uncomfortable position of standing on his head. He was but trying to point to the place where his head had been cast by his murderer, and made his appeal to the living.

(*Written by James W. Harry*)

John Bryarly who owned the mill mentioned above was the father of Robert Bryarly, who was the ancestor of the Lees, Munnickhuysens and others.

"Historic Conowingo" written by Hugh A. Jones (about 1908).

Few people are familiar with the fact of what an important part Conowingo bridge and its elder sister, the Rock Run bridge have played in the politics, as well as the commerce of a vast section of this country. These two bridges spanned a familiar stream. Five hundred miles long, it is only five miles navigable and with its rugged, stony bottom which exists nearly its entire length, dashing waters which in flood time become an overwhelming torrent, due to the rapid fall in the surface of the country, the Susquehanna forms an almost complete barrier to transit between the sections through which it flows, except where spanned by bridges. For the past fifty years Conowingo has been the only passenger bridge on the stream from its mouth to Columbia, some thirty miles above. True, at Peach Bottom a placid portion of the river is crossed by a primitive ferry boat, but its commerce is extremely limited in volume and character.

The first company for the construction of a bridge across the lower Susquehanna, known as the "Rock Run Bridge and Banking Company" was incorporated in 1808, and this charter was substantially amended by an act of the Legislature in 1812. It is worthy of note in this connection, that this charter was finally utilized for the building of the Conowingo bridge many years later. Work was begun on this structure in 1813 and it was completed and opened for travel in 1818, becoming a great thoroughfare between the North and South. Its importance can be the more fully realized when we recall that the Philadelphia and Washington

(Written by Hugh A. Jones)

Railroad was not built and opened for travel until the
Fourth of July, 1837 and did not have any bridge on
which to cross the river until 1868. We do not find
that the banking feature of this Company was ever
availed of, and in 1854 one span was carried down by
the dangerous rhythmic motion incidental to a drove of
cattle being carried across too rapidly. Some of the
cattle were killed in the disaster and it is recalled how
one of the leading citizens of Harford today, but then a
young man, "To fame and fortune still unknown,"
secured and personally dressed the carcass of a handsome bullock for a nominal consideration which furnished his home an ample supply of succulent beef for
months to come. The uninjured cattle were cared for
overnight by Hugh Jones, who on the following morning
piloted them across the river at the "Old Bald Friar"
ferry, one and a half miles above the site of Conowingo
Bridge on the route where Lafayette crossed with his
army during the Revolutionary War, and many more
droves of cattle crossed there until late in the Fall.
The bridge was soon repaired, but an unprecedented
freshet in 1847, the national sequel of the unprece-
dentedly severe Winter of '56–'57 carried away the
structure and from that time on the crumbling piers
have been the only monuments of its past glory.

The origin of Conowingo bridge is veiled somewhat
in mystery and tradition entangles it more or less with
its sister bridge seven miles downstream. It seems to
have been constructed under the charter of 1808 before
referred to and was built by a Contractor named
Wormwag and was operated until 1846 when it was
carried away by the May freshet so common in this
great stream.

This freshet also badly wrecked the Tidewater and
Susquehanna Canal which had been completed in 1839

(*Written by Hugh A. Jones*)

and had already proven very valuable for the transportation of freight as well as to bring to tidewater the coal and lumber of central Pennsylvania.

A party by the name of Henry Wesley at the time of its loss held a mortgage thereon for $1500.00, and some little time later he foreclosed, thus acquiring full ownership of the company's property, which included its piers, terminal facilities, rights of way, etc. These he sold to the new company for $500 cash and $1000 in stock of the new company.

The community feeling the disastrous effect of the bridge's loss, just the same as the people of the same section are feeling today, an act to incorporate the Conowingo Bridge Company was passed in 1847, which among other things provided for the right to raise by subscription in shares of $20 each, the capital stock not to exceed $60,000. The incorporators of the new Company were John Kirk, president; Henry McVey, Absalam Roman, Henry Wesley, and William B. Bond who also acted as its directors. The new Company immediately purchased of Mr. Wesley the old site and all of his rights connected therewith. Evidently it was not an easy matter to place the stock of the new company, for the structure was not begun until the Spring of 1858 and completed in the Spring of 1859. During the freshet of 1865 the Easternmost span of this bridge was carried away on the 18th of March; the upper portion of one of the piers not having been properly constructed (crib work) so that when the end of the bridge was lifted from the pier by the water, it became easy prey to the raging torrent, and this experience was again repeated in February 1904 when the two spans East of the island were lifted from their resting places and carried down the stream. They were promptly replaced by iron spans, which still remain.

(Written by Hugh A. Jones)

In 1861 the war came on and Conowingo plays no small part in the enactment of the thrilling experiences and harrowing scenes of that troubled period. Upon the breaking out of the war, so strong was the sympathy in Maryland for the Confederacy that Captain Steven S. Johns, who at that time lived near Berkley, was able to take possession of and guard the West Entrance of the bridge in order to prevent the passage of Federal soldiers. Later a portion of the 18th Connecticut was stationed for three years in this vicinity, and it was diligently engaged in capturing deserters and sending them as prisoners to the fort near Baltimore.

When Harry Gilmore made his celebrated raid and the railroad bridge was burned across the Gunpowder River, 3000 Federal soldiers, enlisted for a period of thirty days, were hurried to Conowingo and there stationed to cut off the enemy's passage. Foraging and plundering the country thereabouts, they made themselves singularly comfortable while playing soldier. Indeed after the battle of Gettysburg in 1864, Milroy whose division of the Federal army never stopped retreating until it reached Philadelphia, took his wagon train across the Conowingo bridge and later, when moving Southward again, liberally appropriated whatever private property might be convenient for his use, and he even entered uninvited the home of the writer located nearby and ate the steaming dinner prepared for the family. When Captain Johns could no longer hold the fort, tradition says that Squire James Cummings with a keg of powder located on the span, near the middle of the bridge and connected with the shore by means of a train of coal oil, held himself ready on a moment's notice, if Confererate Soldiers did reach that span, to precipitate them into the seething waters of this well-known maelstrom. Later when fearing their

(Written by Hugh A. Jones)

inability to hold the bridge against a Confederate attack, the Federal Soldiers cut all the lateral bracing in the span which stretched across "Job's Hole," so that an army innocent of the fact would be precipitated into the river.

The saddest part of our tale is to be told when we recall the destruction of the bridge by fire on the 6th of June 1907, since which time its handsome stone piers and the two iron spans before mentioned and two wooden spans are the only reminders of this important highway. We use the word *important* intentionally because since the completion of the Columbia and Port Deposit Railway about thirty years ago, and the loss of the Tidewater Canal in 1894, this bridge has been the only means of emptying into the marts of trade the agricultural products from the fertile bosom of Eastern Harford County for many miles around. The burden thus entailed upon these people cannot be over-estimated and they are eagerly waiting for the recon-struction of the bridge under the contract mutually entered into between the old company and the new bridge company incorporated by the Legislature in the winter of 1907.

Signed HUGH A. JONES

From Johnston's History of Cecil County.—"The incorporators of the 1808 Company were as follows: James Sewall, Adam Uhann, Henry W. Physic, William Hollingsworth, Thomas W. Veazey, and Thomas Williams. They were authorized to raise $250,000 by subscription in shares of $50 each, for the building of the bridge at Rock Run. This act failed, as the sub-scriptions could not be collected. New commissioners were appointed to lay out a route for the bridge, which they did, but the route was too long. Eight years

(Written by Hugh A. Jones)

elapsed, and a Company was formed with an amend-
ment in 1816, to allow the company to do its own banking. This was successful. A site was chosen which was
only 20 feet less than a mile long; also four acres of land
on the Cecil end was condemned for stone for the piers.
This bridge was finished in 1818. At this time, John
Archer was president and Thomas L. Savin was cashier
of the Company. The bridge was built by contract by
a Mr. Burr and was burnt 1823, by friction of an iron
shod sleigh. The bridge was rebuilt in 1829–30 by a
Mr. Wormwag, and remained standing, until 1854
when one span was broken down by a drove of cattle
running across. It was never repaired and the remainder was carried away in 1857."

In Mr. Hugh A. Jones' paper I cannot reconcile the
statement that the Conowingo bridge was operated up
to 1846 and that Mr. Henry Weslay had a mortgage
on it, with the statement that the second Rock Run
bridge according to Johnston's History, was rendered
useless in 1854. How could two poor counties afford
two bridges, over the river at the same time. I do not
believe there was anything built at Conowingo until
1858, and that Wesley's mortgage and rights, were on
the other bridge, which Mr. Jones does not mention.

Underground Railway.—Liberty is exemplified pure
and simple in the unconfined maniac, unhampered by
control or inhibitions and liberty as such all will agree
to be of questionable value. On the other hand if we
load a man with chains, he is really no more a slave than
the man loaded with inhibitions. When Lincoln gave
the negro freedom during the Civil War, he did not by
and large, free him from hard work or mental misery,
but by placing his destiny in his own hands, he liber-
ated his will, without which lasting happiness seems to
be impossible. Fifty years previous to the Civil War,

the Society of Friends became aware of this state of affairs and urged its members to free their slaves, which they largely did, and members of their Society were therefore indefatigable in aiding the runaway slaves in their dash for freedom to Canada. This movement for freedom by the slaves was of slow growth, perhaps increasing with the gradual failure of the economic system in the South. At all events more and more slaves slipped across the border each year and they were numbered by the thousands, but it was not until the passage of the Fugitive Slave Law in 1850 that the situation was brought forcibly to the attention of the Nation as a whole. Vigilance Committees were organized in many Cities and hideouts and funds made available for the fugitives, who were constantly passing North towards Canada. Routes were determined and Stations prepared along the way where Colored people could be cared for and aided.

As a rule the escaping slave had to depend on himself and the North Star until he reached the Pennsylvania or Ohio line and then singly or in batches of from fifteen or twenty they were passed on in covered carriages or under straw in farm wagons. The fare from Baltimore to York, Pennsylvania was forty dollars as the risk was high, particularly after the passage of the Fugitive Slave Law. Thomas Garrett, a Friend living in Wilmington Delaware, was finally arrested and forced to pay a heavy fine for his abolitionist practices, although even this did not deter him from constant efforts along these lines.

My own grandfather was twice arrested for helping slaves in Philadelphia, but nothing could be proved against him. Many slaves crossed from Maryland into Gettysburg and York, which were the nearest stations to the border. Some of these slaves would be sent to Harrisburg and some to Columbia where they would be hidden by the Quakers and then passed on by night. So great was the exodus at Columbia that slave owners posted men along the route and paid teamsters to give information, but all to no avail.

In our part of Harford County, one of the routes across the river was at Worthington's Landing. The road leading down to it may be seen today as it descends the river hill immediately below the Conowingo power house. William Worthington lived in the house recently owned by Edward S. Shure, since torn down, and in the evening frequently one of his men would come to him and whisper, "Uncle Billy there's people on the hill," thereupon Uncle Billy would order a sheep killed and cooked for the escaping slaves then hiding in the cornfields, and after dark a boat would be available at the landing to take them across the river. A colored man by the name of Had Harris undertook this service. His house formerly stood beside the canal and near the recent paper mill.

The accounts of the escape of slaves, and I have hundreds of them, are essentially alike. They "Just got tired of it." One slave at least, escaped from the Hayes property at Shuck's Corner and several others left the farm of Dr. Abraham Street near the Rocks. Their mistresses were the worst offenders as a rule, and many of them showed little mercy.

Indian Contemporaries.—There is a curious, though rather gruesome tale told by the descendants of William Stephenson and occurring around 1790. At this time there lived on a small rocky knoll, a quarter of a mile below the dwelling of the above mentioned William Stephenson, an Indian, one of the last remaining along the lower river. He made a habit during the later years of his life of coming to the house once or twice a day for scraps of food. On one occasion he failed to make his appearance, and on investigation his body was discovered in the hut partially devoured by hogs which ran at large in the woods. The body was taken up and buried so it is said, in the family grave-yard nearby.

Another Indian, known locally as "Basket Maker Will," dwelt in a "lean-to" under a large rock and behind the present dairy barn of Mr. Johns Hopkins at Darlington. He is said to have occupied this site about 1830.

These rambling Sketches of Harford County now come to an end and if they have been instrumental in helping others preserve the vanishing past of this our most beautiful County, I shall feel fully repaid for my labor

FINIS